BEDTIME STORIES
of the
Ingleside Inn

by Mel Haber

FOREWORD

For You, Our Special Guest,

Many people have asked me over the past years how I came to buy the Inn, how it got started as a hotel or restaurant, my background, etc. I hope you will enjoy reading the "hows, wherefores and whatevers." I have had so many interesting and humorous adventures in my restaurant and hotel career that any attempt to keep track of them all would be impossible. At the very beginning I made an attempt to find any books that had been written by restaurateurs or hoteliers recalling their experiences, and to my amazement found out that there were none written. There had been books written about hoteliers and restaurateurs, but none by them, on some of the adventures they were sure to have had. My only explanation for that would be that the intellect of the average hotelier and restaurateur is not one of an author.

I truly hope you enjoy reading these stories as much as I enjoyed living them. So many of you are part of the Ingleside Inn's inception, progress and success that I want to extend my personal thanks to you for helping me make it what it is today, a very special place for very special people.

Mel Haber

Lord John Press
19073 Los Alimos Street
Northridge, California 91326

ISBN: 0-935716-89-0

Bedtime Stories
of the
Ingleside Inn

by

Mel Haber

Lord John Press, 1988
Northridge, California

Brooklyn Discovers
Palm Springs

NUMBER ONE
IN A SERIES
OF ONE MILLION

It was a Saturday morning about noon, March of 1975, and I was just hanging around my Palm Springs condominium. A fellow I knew who worked at one of the hotels in Palm Springs dropped by and suggested we take a ride. I was wearing my standard Palm Springs uniform which consisted of, sneakers with no socks, cut-off dungarees, and a T-shirt. We piled into his old convertible and started to drive through town. He mentioned some property that he felt his boss should look at, and asked me if I would be interested in driving through it. Having absolutely nothing else to do, I said "sure."

I was surprised to discover the property was virtually only two blocks from the center of town. We entered through a pair of iron gates and lo and behold, there was this charming private estate sitting in the center of town. The entire property was secluded behind high walls. A large, circular driveway took you through it and out a gate at the other side. The first thing you saw when you entered was a charming, Spanish-style hacienda, complete with tiled roofs and lovely vines on the wall. It was about two acres of land in a park-like setting, and in addition to the main hacienda, there were several Spanish-style bungalows situated lazily around the property. There was a large veranda extending the length of the main building, and three people were seated there. It was a scene out of old-world Spain, or perhaps even Mexico. My first impression was that the world had somehow forgotten about this property, and neglected to build the office building or stores that belong to such a great location. The property had charm and atmosphere as only a piece of property could have that was built many years before.

As we drove through the two acres, I was really impressed with the charm and beauty of the place. It was obvious that it was suffering from neglect, and it needed a great deal of rejuvenation, but the intrinsic charm could not be denied. My friend asked if I would like to stop and look inside, and I said "sure." At this point I was thrilled just to have something to do for a couple of hours.

We took a tour of the main building. The interior looked like an old European inn, and was even more charming than the exterior. First we went through the Lobby, which had a large fireplace built into the wall. There were high ceilings from which hung chandeliers, and what seemed like very valuable pieces of furniture were scattered about. There was a registration desk, and a gentleman came out from behind it and introduced himself as the manager. He said he was representing the owner who was totally inactive and anxious to sell the property. He didn't sound like a Californian and was obviously an Easterner. Upon chatting with him, I discovered he was from the "Borscht Belt." This is the Catskill Mountain region in New York State with which I was very familiar having worked there as a teenager. It was a kind of haven for Jewish people with money. He was definitely Jewish, and this was significant only in light of the past history of the Ingleside Inn. He told us that it was originally a private estate, and was turned into a hotel in 1935. He explained that from the first day and up to the present time, it was totally anti-Semitic almost to an extreme. The present owner was of substantial wealth from San Francisco. He had been a former guest of the woman who originally made it into a hotel. She had run it very successfully for 30 years, catering only to the blue bloods of the world, and discriminating against everyone other than the pure "WASPS." Fascinated by the history he was unraveling, we sat down on the beautiful veranda, and he filled us in with more details.

He told me the Inn was originally built as a private estate in 1925 by the widow of the man who manufactured the Pierce Arrow Motorcar. It was sold in 1935 to a woman from Indiana. She ran it for the next 30 years as a very personal, private "Club," and had people come primarily by invitation. She lived on the property, and personally catered to their every need. She gave everyone staying at the Inn more of a feeling of being invited to someone's home rather than staying in a hotel. She was extremely successful in getting the clientele she wanted, and her roster of former guests reads like the Who's Who of the world...presidents, royalty, and captains of industry stayed at the hotel and enjoyed this lady's hospitality. The manager explained the hotel was loaded with antiques gathered by the original owner on special buying trips to Europe. He said that the value of the antiques in the hotel were probably more than the asking price of the entire piece of property. When the woman passed away in 1965, one of her regular guests, a very substantial man from a banking family in San Francisco, bought the Inn in the hope of carrying on in the same tradition. However, he was totally inactive and absent for the greater part of the ten years he owned it, and lost a great deal of money operating it in absentia. He had presently taken sick and was most anxious to sell the property, even though he loved it dearly. The gentleman we were talking to was hired to run the property until a buyer could be found. The manager dropped a few names of people who had stayed at the Inn such as Howard Hughes, J.C. Penney, Krupp of the German munitions family, Giannini who built and owned the Bank of America, Lily Pons who had lived there for 13 years, and on and on and on...I was absolutely fascinated by the story. He then asked us if we would like to see the restaurant, which we didn't even know existed. He took us down to a little house at the end of the property, and when we walked in, I couldn't believe my eyes.

It was about 12:30 in the afternoon, approximately 90–95 degrees outside. My friend and I were dressed in cut-off dungarees and sneakers with T-shirts, and as we opened the restaurant door, lo and behold, there were twenty couples sitting there having lunch. The average age of the people sitting there would be around 70 years, I guess. Every lady was dressed "for tea" with long dresses and every man was wearing a jacket and tie. I commented to the manager that I felt awfully warm, and he said there was *no air-conditioning.* My thoughts were that this was either a stage-setting and they were shooting a movie, or these people were dead and forgot to fall over! I could't believe my eyes. If I were going to set the stage for a meeting of the Daughters of the American Revolution, or the Sons of the Original Settlers of America, I could not have done a better job.

The restaurant was decorated in rose-colored flocked wallpaper, with burgundy drapes and burgundy carpeting. The waiters had a look about them as if they belonged, and the only thing I could find missing from the whole picture was the strolling violinist. The contrast between the Jewish manager I was talking to, and the obviously Wasp-ish clientele struck me as a pre-arranged comedy routine. He greeted a few of the people very politely in soft tones of voice, of course, and I wasn't sure whether this thing was on the level, a comedy routine, or someone was just trying to drive me mad.

I couldn't wait to get out of there because I never felt more out of place in my life. The manager then suggested showing me several of the hotel rooms. Each room was different, but they all had a similar feeling to my grand-mother's living room back in New York. The only way I could describe this whole experience is to say it was absolutely "trippy." I really felt I had been transported back one hundred years. He showed me two different basements (a rarity in Palm Springs) where I relished looking at what appeared to be valuable old pieces of furniture, newspapers, draperies, etc. Kiddingly I asked if this did not originally belong to the Collier Brothers (they were very famous wealthy recluses in New York and when they died, and their apartment was searched, it was discovered they had never thrown anything away in their entire lives). He showed us fifteen full drawers of index cards on former guests. I thumbed through some of them and actually got goose pimples. The names I ran across were legendary to me. I found a registration card on Salvador Dali, the famous artist on which had been penciled "I believe he is a painter!!!" There was one for Elizabeth Taylor that said "Movie Actress" with several question marks after it. There was a card for Mr. and Mrs. Samuel Goldwyn of Hollywood, California, and some-one had penciled in "No Good. They're Jewish." A card read "Earl Martyn," and penciled alongside it was "Howard Hughes, wants no one to know."

At this point I must explain something about myself. Number One, I had just sold a piece of real estate and was looking to reinvest the money in another piece of real estate. Number Two, throughout my entire life I have been presented with thousands of different business proposi-tions. I had *never heard* a business proposition that didn't sound good to me. By this time two hours had passed, and I was foaming at the bit to buy this property. I was sure that after I owned it I would find the treasure of Sierra Madre buried in the ground on the property.

It made me think of a story my father used to tell me about the two peddlers on the East side of New York who had men's clothing stores. What they would do was to take a piece of paper that felt like money, fold it up and leave it in one of the pants pockets amongst the suits they were selling. When a customer would try on the suit and put his hand in the pocket, he would feel the "money" there, assume that someone who had tried on the suit had left the money by mistake. They would quickly buy the suit only to find they had been duped. I wasn't sure I was being baited, or whether this whole situation was real. The asking price on the property was, I felt, very realistic for the land value alone.

My tendency my whole life had been to act first and think later. My friend left and the manager and I sat down. Quickly I made an offer 25% under what he was asking (this method always made me feel I was getting a bargain, and people who knew my routine would simply mark up what they were trying to sell me by 30%, so that I would be allowed to play my game and win). He said my offer was ridiculous, and that the property was worth every dime of the asking price. My heart was palpitating and my brain was spinning so fast I was beginning to get a headache. I suggested I come over the following morning at 10 o'clock and have coffee with him, and see if we could work something out. He came up with the standard seller's comment which was that if I were seriously interested, I would have to move fast because there were several other people interested in the property and he would probably be selling it in a couple of days. His comment had the desired psychological effect. Immediately I experienced panic and anxiety over the possibility of losing the deal. His statement seemed to work, and by the time I left I was promising him a rather large commission if I got the property at my price. He said I was in luck since this was the weekend and nothing could transpire until we met again. I thanked my lucky stars for this piece of good fortune. I left, pacified that he would be *kind enough* to let me buy the place and not sell it to someone else.

I did not sleep all that night, contemplating the many possibilities of the Ingleside Inn. With my vast knowledge of the restaurant and hotel business, WHICH WAS ZERO, I started to scheme every angle I could as to what I would do with the property. The manager had told me that the overhead, including mortgage, utilities, the gardeners, and the chef was approximately $5,000 a month. My first thought was to find four friends and buy the property as partners. We would draw lots for blocks of four rooms each; (the property had 20 rooms) we would then each own 20% of the property. We would have our own private dining room, our own chef. It seems a lot better than buying five separate condominiums. We would then have the right to do anything we liked with our four rooms. We could either combine them to make one luxurious suite for ourselves, or keep them as four separate rooms and have relatives and friends use them as they saw fit. That was Number One idea. The second idea I thought of was to turn it into a health club, what is commonly known as the Fat Farm, for women. Two acres in a magnificent setting in the middle of Palm Springs is a natural for women to use while their husbands are playing golf. My mind was flitting feverishly. As I look back, it is interesting *that at no point* did I consider leaving it a restaurant and hotel which it already was.

By 10 o'clock the following morning, I had driven through the property thirteen times and each time had different ideas as to what I was going to do with it. At 10 o'clock I was waiting anxiously on the veranda for the manager to appear. He showed up at five minutes after ten, we exchanged good mornings, and went into the restaurant to have a cup of coffee. As soon as we were seated, a young man appeared at the table. He seemed to be about twenty years old, stood about 5'11", weighed approximately 150 pounds, and when he spoke to the manager, his thick, Southern drawl was, I guessed, from the Ozark area. He was wearing a shirt and tie which was certainly a rarity in Palm Springs, especially in the morning. The manager introduced him as bellman, bookkeeper, desk clerk and assistant manager of the Ingleside Inn. The manager gave him some instructions, and he left. The manager then explained that the young man was his assistant. He paid him $300 a month, plus room and board. The young fellow worked approximately twenty hours a day, seven days a week, performing all the various functions. We continued discussing the Inn when I noticed a middle-aged woman picking flowers in the garden of the restaurant. The manager informed me she was the housekeeper, maid and secretary. He said that between the young boy and the woman, the three of them ran the entire property. He pointed out that the restaurant had its own staff consisting of a chef, who had been working on the property for twenty years, one woman who helped him, and four funny little waiters who would have looked right at home in an English drawing room.

The hotel had always been on what is commonly known as the American plan, which means that hotel guests receive three meals a day included in the price of the room. The dining room was closed to the public, and it was quite an honor for an outside guest to be invited to dine there. There was no liquor license, so the guests would bring their own bottle with their name taped on it, and that was their private stock for their stay. This arrangement made the people staying at the Inn feel that they were guests in someone's home. The woman who owned the place would preside over the meals as hostess. She had named the restaurant after the chef. As the manager gave me some of the colorful background of the Inn, it became obvious that anything of consequence took place between 1935 and 1965, the period this woman owned it. He alluded to the great, interesting history of the Inn, and its former guests. We spent an hour structuring several offers for the owner. I used every bit of persuasion I could summon up to convince him to make sure I got the place, and finally the key to the deal was simply to promise him he could stay on as manager and live there. With that extra bonus, he assured me he would drive to Rancho Santa Fe where the owner lived, and personally appeal to him on my behalf.

He called the owner and made an appointment to see him that evening with the offer. I assured him I would stay over until Monday, so we could open escrow if my offer were accepted. That evening about 10 o'clock, I got the call that I had the deal. Then I proceeded to get butterflies in my stomach and a nervous headache. I slept restlessly that night and Monday morning I opened escrow to buy the Ingleside Inn.

Looking back in retrospect, I could have no idea as to how that day would affect the rest of my life.

NOW WHAT???

I now owned the Inn and a restaurant called "Orville's," named after the chef who had been there so long. I had inherited along with the hotel, a staff consisting of a funny-looking 45-year-old fat man with a limp, a toupee and a very Jewish demeanor, who was my manager; a 20-year-old boy from Arkansas with an incredible drawl who was my Bell Captain, bellman, bookkeeper, front desk clerk; a chef who was temperamental, totally absorbed with pornography, and who had never cooked for more than 50 people at a time; a lovely housekeeper who picked fresh flowers for the rooms, but who had a bad back and had difficulty making beds, and four little 60-year-old waiters, one of whom was an Englishman who called everyone 'Mum' and 'Dad,' with the net results that most customers were offended.

In the short period of a week, between the time I found the Ingleside Inn and closed the deal, I had approached the only three people I knew in California to go partners with me. Their response was unanimously 'no' for varying reasons. One had sent an expert friend of his to look at the property and evaluate it. He concluded it had no chance because it only had 20 rooms. Another friend from Los Angeles drove down and responded I was crazy. "What do you see in the property anyway?" he asked me. Another friend had no money. I couldn't help but feel they thought I was nuts. Nevertheless, I went straight ahead. One of the guys who turned me down was, at this point, my closest friend. It was Bobby who had a house in Palm Springs where I used to spend every weekend before I bought my condominium. By a simple process of elimination, because I knew no one else in Palm Springs, he became my confidante and advisor.

Now I started to deal with the realities of my folly. My first concern was to find someone who could manage the property and at least maintain the small amount of income it was generating. I was content to leave the manager I had inherited there, but I wanted someone, in addition, to be my representative as business commitments in Los Angeles precluded my spending a great deal of time in Palm Springs. Bobby and I were having coffee in his house one morning, when he suggested a certain "local Baptist" minister as the ideal manager. It seemed with that background I would at least get an "honest shake." Although I had made a deal with Morris, the manager, who came with the property, I felt I needed my *own* man in there. I would leave Morris with the responsibility of running it on a day-to-day basis, but I wanted someone there full-time to represent me.

A meeting was set up, and based on my history of hiring *everyone* I ever interviewed I made a deal with my new General Manager, Luther, the Baptist minister-manager. He had a background of a general contractor and he would be in charge of construction, decorating, controlling the money, and relieving Morris when necessary. The contrast between the tall, lean, slow-walking (with a drawl no less) Baptist minister, and the short, fat Jewish guy with a limp and toupee, was something to behold.

My entire staff was now rounded out. The only problem was that this crew of misfits would have been more appropriate for a slapstick comedy than a hotel and restaurant. Now that I owned this hotel and restaurant in Palm Springs, had my crew together, I had no idea what to do next. My whole life, the pattern had been the same. First I spend a great deal of time and effort digging myself into a big hole. *Then I spend a great deal of time and effort digging myself out of the big hole.* If I were successful, I would eventually wind up exactly where I started. From all reports I got, Barron Hilton was not in the least scared about my entry into the hotel industry.

Now that I was a hotel owner, I started to formulate ideas and plans. I honestly don't remember at what point I decided to keep it as a hotel and restaurant, but felt that with minor improvements I could keep it going the way it was, and even generate a little profit until I had more concrete ideas. My Baptist-manager's experience as a general contractor would help to implement the work that had to be done. I didn't have a great deal of money to spend, and my friend Bobby volunteered to help me decorate the property. He prided himself on being very artistic and creative.

Bobby lived with a girlfriend, Judy, in Palm Springs. She was a nice girl, quite content to spend her entire life in their Palm Springs home shuffling from the bedroom to the kitchen and back to the bedroom. If Judy never had to get dressed or go outside, that would be just fine with her. Bobby had a pattern similar to mine. He went to Los Angeles during the week for business. He was a salesman, and he returned every weekend to Palm Springs and Judy. I put Bobby in charge of decorating the property.

When he came down on Fridays, he would collect his girlfriend, come over to the hotel and start barking orders; "Judy, paint this trim, mirror the ceiling, make a built-in over this wall, get a flowered spread," etc., etc. His lady would sit like a secretary taking notes as he barked orders with all the authority in the world. He would spend about two or three hours doing this. He reminded me of a general issuing battle plans.

He would then march off quite content with himself. It was almost as if *all he had to do* was to say it, for it to be done. I would sit in awe watching his creativity flow. After these sessions were over, reality would set in, and I would start to wonder how all these directives would be accomplished, and how much they would cost. As they left, his lady would always give me that puzzled look as if to say "What happens now?" Whether his plans could be carried out, or whether they would be economically feasible never seemed to enter his mind. This went on every Friday and Saturday for about six weeks. On Mondays we would return to Los Angeles, and his girlfriend would return to her very contented life-style of doing no more than shuffling from her bedroom to the kitchen and back again. On certain days of the week she didn't even do that. She simply spent the whole day in her bedroom.

Two months passed by, of the same procedure, and my Baptist-minister-manager started to tear apart the rooms so that my friend's idea could be implemented. Suddenly one day it dawned on me that not only had nothing been done, but I was worse off than when I started. Six rooms which had been shabby but rentable had now been torn apart, and a great deal of money had been spent. Nothing had been planned, ordered or done to get them back into shape although the girlfriend had about 50 pages of notes. During the same period of time, I was very busy in Los Angeles formulating plans and ideas. I was working on brochures, a logo, stationery, where-to-buy toilet paper and towels wholesale, merchandising ideas, etc. My consultant-advisor-friend Bobby had put me in touch with a well-known public relations firm in Beverly Hills, that had a clientele that could run the Academy Awards without any outsiders. They had condescended to accept me as a client because I was a friend of Bobby's. This was my first contact with a public relations firm and, based on their fee, I knew my hotel would be as famous as the Waldorf-Astoria in a short period of time. I met with them at least twice a week and discussed the various items I would need. I was primarily looking for a color scheme, and a "look" for stationery, napkins, matches, etc., for an area of identification with the public. My one and only contribution to the physical improvement of the Ingleside Inn was the idea that it was absolutely essential to add a jacuzzi to the property. My manager assured me that he could have done that without any problem.

As the weeks passed, more and more of my time and brain power was devoted to this project. The feeling was that things were happening. Bobby and Judy were decorating the place, the manager was having the jacuzzi built, and the PR firm was working on a logo and theme. I was personally very busy writing orders for "toilet paper and soap."

Over the next two months I came down to Palm Springs every Thursday evening and spent Friday and Saturday with Bobby and Luther, the minister-manager, reviewing that week. All day Sunday would be spent organizing my notes and making lists to be accomplished in Los Angeles the coming week. Mondays I would return to Los Angeles and try to conduct some of my regular business where, incidentally, I was MAKING A LIVING! Running the automotive novelty business I was in was interwoven with my meetings with my PR firm and different toilet paper salesmen.

My weekend meetings in Palm Springs were always held in a corner table in the restaurant. This was primarily because in every movie I had ever seen the owner had his special table, and there always appeared to be an endless flow of people to it. I enjoyed playing this role.

The two months passed very quickly, and I decided it was time to regroup. I planned a series of meetings for the coming weekend to see where everything stood. It seemed like a number of things were in process, but nothing was getting accomplished. I had already gone through quite a sum of money, and I was getting scared that things were out of hand. I had paid the PR agency for two months and so far received *nothing*. From Day One, I had insisted that in order to capture the charm of the place they had to personally see it, but at this point they had not done so. The head man finally agreed to meet me in Palm Springs on Saturday. From Los Angeles I telephoned my generals and set up separate times and meetings with each one for that weekend.

Saturday morning at approximately 10 a.m., the public relations guy arrived and I promptly took him on a tour of the facilities. We spent about 45 minutes looking at everything and then sat down to a cup of coffee. He said he had put a lot of thought into making this project successful. I was anxious for the great words that were going to make me a millionaire. I waited anxiously to hear these great words to come from the creative genius who was to make me successful. He spoke very slowly, for dramatic presentation. He said, "Mel, we've got to keep this property clean. *I noticed several things around I could point out to you such as cigarette butts, discarded papers, etc.!"*

After regaining my composure, I assured him I was aware of the importance of what he was saying, and the astuteness of his observation, and apologized explaining that we were renovating and therefore changing everything. I was too frustrated to say anything else and simply told him I would call him in Los Angeles during the week, thanking him profusely for coming down and especially for the profound piece of advice. He left with a feeling of being truly appreciated.

The next meeting on the agenda was one with Morris, the Resident Manager. During this two-month period, the hotel and restaurant had been functioning and doing a relatively small amount of business. The best I could determine was that I had *a partner of whom I was unaware*. It slowly dawned on me that when my receipts were $700 in the restaurant, somehow only $350 wound up in the bank. I did not know whether I really had a right to complain as *at least* he was fair enough to split it down the middle. My meeting with Morris provided no answers...only a hurt look on Morris's face. He said he couldn't explain the missing money because Luther was the general manager. There was no doubt that Morris was not a member of the Brotherhood of Christian and Jews. So far I had accomplished nothing, and couldn't wait to have a meeting with Luther. I had about half an hour to kill, so I started wandering around the property making notes. I wandered over to my pride and joy, my new jacuzzi. It was not quite finished, but I noticed a serious crack in the bottom. Luther and I sat down to coffee, and reviewed some of the work in progress. At my friend Bobby's direction, six rooms had been torn apart but Luther wasn't quite sure what came next. The jacuzzi was coming along nicely, and between the electric and pool work it would probably run ONLY ABOUT $50,000. Luther said if I didn't have his expertise, it would have cost $65,000. I couldn't believe my ears. The jacuzzi was worth—tops—$15,000. I then questioned him about the missing revenue, and he said that probably Morris had taken it. He apologized for having to run but he had some important business to take care of at the church. I was left sitting in a coma; I felt like screaming but did not want to alarm the six customers I had in the restaurant. WHAT THE HELL HAD I GOTTEN MYSELF INTO??? After staring into space for about an hour, I came to a decision. The reality that struck the hardest, was the fact that I'd have to give up a paycheck which had been my security for 22 years. No matter what other business deals I'd been involved in, the regular paycheck had always been there. Now I would have to give up my job that I had had for 22 years and move to Palm Springs, in order to protect my investment. On July 4, 1975, I packed my car and moved to Palm Springs to launch a new career and a new life.

The first thing I learned about Palm Springs was that the weather was so hot in the summer that there was little in the way of business for a hotel/restaurant operation. In those days the Inn had no air-conditioning, so I closed the place with the intention of carrying out renovations during the summer in order to open in September, in time for the season. I fired Luther, my Baptist-minister-manager, as I could not afford an unknown partner. As I had discovered, he had been helping himself to a percentage of whatever business was coming in.

There was a carpenter working around the place, a man from Mississippi, in his middle forties and in the absence of anyone else, I hired him to be the foreman for the renovation work. Also, I engaged the services of two young lady decorators from Los Angeles, a decision based on their reasonable fee rather than any proven ability at their profession.

Soon I was totally absorbed in the project and came to realize that there was an incredible amount of work to be done before opening day. The major projects included: redecorating the dining room, remodeling the kitchen, building a bar and lounge area, renovating all the rooms and restoring the exterior and grounds to a reasonable condition.

As I rushed about each day making lists and formulating ideas, the immensity of the project grew. I had to come up with a marketing program, create a color scheme, create a logo, order endless amounts of printing required by a hotel and restaurant such as menus, postcards, letterheads, brochures, matches, napkins, and so on, as well as making sure all the furniture, drapes, restaurant utensils and the like were taken care of. Finally, Mel Haber had found a project, a single pursuit, that could consume all his energy and time, not to mention money, which was being spent at an incredible rate.

In quick order, I began acquiring staff to work on the project. A friend introduced me to a young chef who was then living at the beach with his wife and baby. Charlie was about twenty-eight, had a jovial expression and a walrus moustache, all of which gave him the general air of what most people would call a "beach bum." He was completely dedicated to the art of preparing fine foods. I hired Charlie, and he offered the services of two friends of his from the beach to help him renovate the kitchen. I took up his offer.

Next, a nineteen-year-old guy walked in looking for work. He said he was capable of carpentry, painting and some electrical work. I hired him, and he became a sort of administrative aide to me. A friend in Los Angeles sent me two young guys named Larry and Skip, who were willing to work as laborers for the summer in return for good sleeping quarters and minimum wages.

Skip was 30, very skinny and balding, and a typical intellectual type. He was attempting manual labor as one of life's great experiences. They were as close as peas in a pod, and I was never able to figure out the attraction. Between them they had the I.Q. of about 60, but they were nice, lovable, fumbling idiots. Whenever they painted a room, they painted themselves in a corner and couldn't get out. It was impossible to explain to them to start at the back of the room and paint their way to the door. For some reason known only to them, they found it easier to start from the moment they walked in, at the threshold of the door, and paint their way back into the room. On the occasions that they went to eat, they would simply walk across the freshly painted floor and across the property to Palm Canyon Drive, to a restaurant to get some food. You never had to wonder where either of them were because the paint on the bottom of their feet would leave a nice, neat trail no matter where they went. If you wanted to find Larry and Skip, you simply went to the lawn area seeking the freshest tracks leading away from the hotel or back towards the hotel. All of the rooms were being painted white so that at the end of four weeks probably the only spot on Skip that wasn't white were his privates. He managed to paint himself from head to toe as well as the rooms. I often wondered if his buddy, Larry, didn't use him as a paint roller.

Paul the architect, had his own thing going. He was obsessed with building tables for the restaurant that consisted of cutting thousands of slats in wood and nailing them together so that you had a table top that consisted of thousands of little pieces of wood nailed together. He was very busy on that project of sawing his wood, nailing it together, and could always be found in a certain spot at any given moment doing just that. I once figured out that if he worked efficiently and diligently for one week, he could finish one table top. The fact that they would ultimately be covered by tablecloths and would not be seen by anybody did not deter him one bit.

The summer of 1975 had no days and no nights. It was one long blur where all I could see was work that never ended. The norm was that every project had to be done over three or four times. A combination of urgency and inefficiency resulted in everything costing twice as much as it should have.

My foreman (the carpenter) set up a command post on the floor of the dining room where he sat next to a telephone and ordered anything the various workers told him they needed. Charlie and his friends from the beach spent all their time ripping out the equipment in the kitchen. It wasn't necessary, but they had the idea that renovation meant pulling things apart so they could be put together again. Being beach types who persisted in going barefoot, they spent a good part of the day removing splinters from their feet.

Jay, the young guy who became my assistant, worked around the clock with me every day, and I came to really respect him. No matter what I needed he would always come up with something. When I arrived at work at three o'clock in the morning, I'd find him asleep on the diving board near the pool. He said it was cooler sleeping outside. His big hassle in life was dealing with Larry and Skip who spent most of their time hiding rather than painting, and were totally useless.

One particular incident sticks out as typical of the entire project. I had arrived at the hotel at approximately 3 a.m., to get my head together and make lists and schedules for the day. That week the emphasis was on building the bar in Melvyn's. I went down to the restaurant area to inspect the progress of the bar itself. I was seated at the bar and, for some reason, I was not able to face where the bartender would be standing. I had never been a great one for bars but I knew that whenever I sat at a bar I was facing the bartender. I was really confused and sat racking my brains as to what was wrong, as my stool was right next to the bar and I could only sit sideways and not face the bartender. It took me an hour and a half to discover that we had forgotten to put the ledge on the bar and consequently, if you were sitting flush against the bar, you had no room to put your legs in front of you and therefore could not face the bartender. Rather than being discouraged that someone had forgotten the ledge, I was excited at finding the solution to the problem in only two hours.

Theoretically, Charlie the chef was in charge of that, and when I confronted him that morning, he had no time to deal with the problem as he was busy moving kitchen equipment around for the third time. I was to discover that Charlie tore the kitchen apart three times and when he ultimately put it back together, he forgot to put back the pantry area without which you cannot function and that is an essential element in a commercial kitchen.

As the month of August started to disappear on us, I had a big pep rally to explain that we had to work harder as Labor Day was quickly approaching. For some reason I had fixed in my mind that Labor Day signaled the beginning of the season, and I was rushing at a frantic pace to be ready, although nobody ever told me that few come to Palm Springs in September, and the menswear convention which had been coming to town for the past twenty years had canceled for the first time in history. The net result was that I spent a lot of extra money and energy and effort to be ready for September, when *nobody would be in town*. I had a meeting with the entire crew to rally their last dying effort to get the Ingleside Inn and Melvyn's Restaurant ready.

Looking at the entire crew assembled, all of whom I loved dearly by this time, I vowed that some day this story would be written, THERE WAS NOT ONE COMPETENT BETWEEN THE LOT and it was a sight to behold seeing them assembled all at one time.

Charlie the chef was busy picking his toenails; Paul the architect looked like he was anxious to get back to nailing his little tables, and Skip was almost invisible seated in the back against the white wall due to the fact he was painted from head to toe and just blended into the wall. Anyway, they all swore their undying dedication and energies to finishing the job in the next few weeks.

Trucks and shipments started to arrive from the decorators, and certain finishing touches were finally being put in place. I cannot describe the elation I felt to see certain things coming to life after all that work.

Over the summer, many locals had stopped by the Inn to see what was happening. The word was all over town that some "slick guy from New York" with plenty of money had taken it over.

I received a lot of advice, opinions and comments. Most of the people knew the Ingleside Inn during its heyday, and were personally acquainted with the previous owner, Ruth Hardy. I had heard many fascinating anecdotes and stories about its history. On many occasions rummaging through the various storage areas on the property, including two basements, I came across interesting old articles, records, documents and so forth, and I promised myself that one day I would go through them thoroughly.

I was able to piece together that many years ago Ruth Hardy had come to Palm Springs from Indiana. She had taken over a small property, ran it for a year or two, and then bought the Ingleside Inn in 1935. From 1935 to 1965, Ruth Hardy somehow managed to establish the Inn as the only place in Palm Springs for the most important people. The Inn operated six months of the year and closed the other six months. She lived on the property and ran the Inn as if the people were house guests, catering to their every whim and desire. With only twenty rooms and a dining room exclusively for hotel guests, she was able to give a very personal feeling to everybody. They were carefully screened for breeding, background and manners, and if they were the slightest bit out of line according to her standards, they were not allowed back. She catered to royalty, presidents, and the top echelon in the arts and professional worlds. Ultimately, Ruth Hardy went on to the City Council in Palm Springs, and was responsible for lighting the palm trees on the main street, Palm Canyon Drive. She passed away in 1965, and the town appropriately honored her memory by naming a Ruth Hardy Park.

The second week in September the Society Editor of the only newspaper in Palm Springs called to tell me she wanted to do a historical article on the Ingleside. It seems that once a year the paper did a progress edition, describing the history and progress of the various towns that comprised the desert community. I was pretty excited, and we made an appointment to meet. The editor showed up on a typically busy day, and my main concern was riding herd on my crew. I had told her on the phone that I had discovered a basement crammed with old papers. I knew this article was going to be important to me, but I had no idea how to sift through these documents. As we were discussing the problem, a tiny lady of about fifty interrupted us to say she would like to speak with me. Over the course of the summer, I was constantly being hassled by people wanting to sell me something such as advertising or services. I explained to the lady that I would be tied up for a while, but she insisted on waiting. I returned to the editor and apologized that I was unable to work with her personally, but would assign someone to help her. I took her into the filthy, cluttered basement and left her with one of the boys to assist her in going through the papers. After totally forgetting the little lady waiting for me in the Lobby, she finally managed to corner me and said, "Mr. Haber, I know you're busy, but I just wanted to introduce myself. My name is Billy Hopkins, and I am Ruth Hardy's niece. I worked on this property for twenty years as her assistant, and if you would ever like to know anything about its history, I would be happy to help you." I could hardly believe it, and had to ask her to repeat herself. Then I literally picked her up and physically carried her into the basement and hollered out, "Look what God sent us!" The editor was as thrilled as I was, especially as she would no longer have to search for the information she wanted.

This incident was going to be typical of the type of good luck and fate I would experience at the Ingleside Inn over the next few years and even to the present day when my particular 'guardian angel' seems to be as interested as ever in Mel Haber and his dreams and aspirations.

SIR JOHN

NUMBER TWO
IN A SERIES
OF ONE MILLION

I had heard about this very wealthy, titled Englishman who had just checked into a local Palm Springs hotel. Somebody mentioned he was unhappy there and was considering checking into the Ingleside Inn. He owned two rare old Rolls Royces that he had brought with him, and I was told that he was quite a colorful person.

It was about 10 o'clock in the morning when two gentlemen entered the lobby. One was about 6′1″, 200 lbs, with a head of beautiful white hair, and appeared to be about 60 years old. Accompanying him was a short, stocky, baldheaded man approximately the same age. The shorter man immediately reminded me of a Nazi general (my only exposure to Nazi generals was those I had seen in World War II movies, however this one was missing the monocle). They were both very well dressed. The larger of the two approached the desk, announced loudly in a very British accent, "My name is *Suh* John and I wish to see the Ownah!"

Overhearing this in my office, I approached the two with outstretched hand and introduced myself. The taller man announced again that he was *Suh* John, and introduced the other gentleman as Colonel Russell Hopf. Sir John said that he wished my very best villa for approximately ONE YEAR!!! He explained that he was presently at another hotel and was leaving because they had the audacity to charge him for a plate of cheese and crackers. He felt this should have been complimentary in view of the money he was spending there. I quickly summoned all my charm and manners in order to handle my first experience with "real nobility!" I showed the two men the best villa in the hotel. Sir John said it would be fine with certain minor improvements. Having just opened the hotel two weeks before, I had never rented this $160.00-a-day villa. Sir John whipped out 20 crisp $100 bills and said to please credit his account with $2000. He then inquired if we could properly care for his two Rolls Royces, feed his "Drivvah" and cater to the little demands made by royalty. After assuring him that the entire staff was at his disposal, we returned to the registration desk. He signed in as Sir John Beech, London, England, and informed me he had been personally knighted by Queen Elizabeth. He casually mentioned he would be traveling a bit, and when his room was vacant we should keep tabs on it for him. He said he would be more than happy to pay for the room, although he would not be there much of the time. Just at that moment the Bell Captain elected to inform me that the hotel limousine had broken down. Upon hearing this, Sir John announced "As long as I will be staying here feel free to use my Rolls Royces for the convenience of your guests." That magnanimous offer floored me, and I remember thanking my lucky stars for sending Sir John to me. After seeing to it that Sir John was moved from his former hotel and settled in comfortably, I immediately called the entire staff together from both the restaurant and hotel. I informed them that we had visiting royalty and that he was to be accorded every courtesy and convenience humanly possible. This business was going to be even more fun than I had anticipated!!!

I arrived at the restaurant at my usual 7:30 p.m., and quickly looked around the dining room for familiar faces. I had two problems when I walked around the restaurant; No. 1, I had no idea what to look for, so I forced my eyes to dart everywhere. (At least my guests would not know that I didn't know what I was doing), and No. 2, being new in town, I knew very few people and felt pretty silly, but in all the movies I have seen, all good restaurateurs walked around all-knowingly, so I felt I might as well play the role. Lo and behold, sitting at the most conspicuous table was

Sir John in a white dinner jacket, with a black velvet bow tie. With him was Colonel Russ Hopf and a woman that I judged to be about 55 years old. I must say that Sir John was a striking man because of his size and that head of white hair. Add to that a loud distinct British accent...put him in a white dinner jacket in an elegant dining room, and you really have a dramatic effect, to say the least. Central casting in Hollywood could not have done better. As I approached the table to say 'hello,' I immediately noticed a bottle of Dom Perignon (but of course!). I was introduced to Irene, Sir John's secretary of 20 years and he invited me to have a glass of champagne with them. Sir John was talking about his experiences during World War II where he played an important part in the CIA, and had been appropriately decorated. I sat through the entire meal with them, fascinated by the stories of intrigue during the war. Everybody in the restaurant noticed Sir John because he spoke in a very loud distinctive voice. After dinner I joined them in the back of the Lounge for an after-dinner drink. I was fascinated when Sir John spoke about his Arabian horses, his turquoise mines in Arizona, the acrimonious divorce he was in the middle of, and his desire to get away from it all in the desert. I went home that night feeling honored to have the likes of Sir John staying in my hotel.

The next three days passed uneventfully with my new, illustrious guest. He took all of his meals in the restaurant and always made his presence known. He was constantly accompanied by his secretary and the Colonel. The third night he was there we were having a drink at the bar when Frank Sinatra walked in. Immediately Sir John ran up to him, shook his hand and reminded Mr. Sinatra that they had met at one of Frank's Command Performances for the Queen of England. Mr. Sinatra acknowledged that fact, was very courteous, and proceeded with his party to the Lounge area. Sir John then described all the brilliant details of that night, emphasizing the fact that whenever he was in England, the Queen always invited him to *all* the Command Performances.

In the few days that Sir John had been at the Ingleside Inn, he managed to make sure that everyone, both employees and customers, were aware of his story. He talked about his illustrious career with the CIA, his being knighted by the Queen of England, his turquoise mines, his stables of Arabian horses and the very unpleasant divorce he was in the midst of. Several times a day people would call me aside and ask me: "Is Sir John for real??"

I satisfied all questions by pointing to his two Rolls Royce cars and mentioning he had paid me in advance, in addition to the fact that Colonel Hopf's constant company seemed to verify his credibility.

During the first ten days, Sir John firmly established himself as visiting royalty, and the word quickly spread that the Ingleside Inn was the place for royalty. As he became more at home, the more of a character he became. He requested 100 sets of hotel stationery so that he could inform all his royal and celebrity friends that the Ingleside Inn was the only place for them. Sensing I was new to the business with no following, he at once took a personal interest and assured me that he would help to make the Ingleside Inn into what I dreamed it to be. Nobody could have been a better goodwill ambassador. Wherever he went, to shops, parties, etc., he would announce he was PERMANENTLY residing at the Ingleside Inn. Sir John, being the dashing and flamboyant character he was, completely took Palm Springs by storm and was invited to almost all of the social events.

Arriving one morning at 6 a.m., I found Sir John swimming in the hotel pool and he informed me that by swimming every day he was able to maintain a body that belied his 72 years. That morning I found a note on my desk to call Colonel Hopf. He answered the ringing phone immediately, and in a rather apprehensive tone, asked if I might be able to take a few minutes out of my busy schedule to have coffee with him. After assuring him that I was never too busy for him (any friend of a $160-a-day long-staying guest was a friend of mine), we made a date for 10 o'clock and at his insistence, at a coffee shop OUTSIDE the Ingleside Inn.

Needless to say, my curiousity was really piqued. At approximately 10 o'clock, Colonel Hopf came striding into Sandy's Coffee Shop in full military stride. After exchanging pleasantries, the Colonel bluntly said, and I quote, "Mel, do you think Sir John is for real?" His question did not fully register immediately. Automatically, I reviewed in my mind my impressions and doubts about Sir John, and the fact that all my doubts were allayed BECAUSE of the constant company of Colonel Hopf, whom I knew from people around town to be *real*. The entire premise of Sir John's credibility had been shaken. It took about two minutes to regain my composure and I brilliantly said, "That's a very strange question coming from you, Colonel." He answered, "Mel, if I wasn't at the point of total frustration, I wouldn't be here right now." He went on to say, "Let me tell you what I know about Sir John. About three weeks ago, somebody told me this titled Englishman had arrived, and was looking to purchase some Rolls Royces. Well, I had these two cars for sale and I phoned him at once and set up an appointment. I went over to meet Sir John and he was living in a magnificent suite. He came outside, looked at the cars, asked me how much I wanted for them, drove each one around the block and then agreed to purchase both of them. He asked me if I would be kind enough to loan him the cars to use until he received the funds from overseas, explaining that the reason he was buying them was to have cars in America to use. Naturally, for an $80,000 deal, I agreed. Each day he gave me another reason as to why the check had not arrived. He explained that he was involved in this divorce proceeding, and that his financial matters were a little bit complicated at the moment. The deal was big enough so that I started to spend all my time with Sir John. As I mentioned, every day he told me a different story, and the last one he's given me is that he is waiting for a key to arrive in the mail for a safety deposit box in Mexico, right over the border. He said that as soon as he gets that key, he and I would drive down to Mexico and pick up the money for the cars. He certainly seems real enough, but I thought perhaps the fact that he has been with you ten days, you might have learned something. Since he has had the cars he has told everybody that they are his, and that he owns them. I am beginning to wonder if he did not use the cars and me to establish himself. In fact, I am beginning to have some doubts about the whole situation."

I now found Sir John even more interesting than before, and assured the Colonel that on the basis of this information, I would look at him with a different perspective and see if I could find out anything that would be of value to the Colonel. I returned to the Ingleside Inn and discussed this situation with my General Manager. It was his point of view that due to the fact that Sir John had put money up front, our exposure was limited, and that we would just have to keep tabs on him.

Another ten days passed and Sir John owed me approximately $2500 more, which we requested and he promptly paid. He informed us that he would be out of town for a few days and to make sure his villa was kept intact. During the several days that Sir John was out of town, many people in the restaurant mentioned that they would love to meet Sir John, if the opportunity presented itself. I assured them that he was around constantly when he was in town, and that there would be no problem.

After approximately 10 days Sir John reappeared on the scene with a seemingly very polite young man, and a brand new Mercedes 450 SL. Sir John introduced the young man as his DRIVER!! His major concern was to make sure that his driver would be able to take his meals with my help. I assured him he would be treated as one of our own, and Sir John suggested that we have a cup of coffee together so he could fill me in with the details of his exciting trip.

We were seated in the corner of the dining room and he proceeded to tell me that the main purpose of his trip out of town was to receive an award for his Arabian horses, and that I should come to his villa and see the beautiful crown they had bestowed on him as the owner of such magnificent animals. Sir John explained that he was finally making progress on his messy divorce, and that his turquoise mines were producing more than ever. He told me that in the short period of time he had been staying at the Ingleside Inn, it was like home to him and it was a great FEELING to be back. He also mentioned that the following day he was going to purchase a large aquarium for the living room of his villa, and he felt that the little pond in our courtyard would look lovely with some exotic fish and insisted on gifting me with them. He was going in to rest for a while, and said he would see me at dinner, and would my lady be free to join us. After checking with her, I told him it would be her pleasure.

About 6 o'clock that evening, Sir John entered the Lounge, beautifully attired in his traditional dinner jacket and velvet bow tie, making his usual striking appearance. He was carrying several gift-wrapped boxes, and he gave one to my manager, one to my son, and one to me, mentioning that he had found this great Mens Shop in town that afternoon, loved the merchandise and had gone on a spending spree. It seems he had purchased about $3,000 worth of clothing on his good name. He fell in love with a certain shirt and felt the important people at the Ingleside Inn should have them as his gift. When my lady appeared, he presented her with a gold goblet, and with all the appropriate pomp and ceremony proclaimed he was "dubbing" her *"Lady Carol,"* and that never again would she drink out of an ordinary glass, but *only* out of this special gold goblet. At this point he really must have had a hell of a trip as his benevolence was overflowing. LADY CAROL and Sir John dined together, and I must tell you, they made a striking couple.

After dinner we all went back to the Lounge to listen to our regular singer, and have our after dinner aperitif. Sir John was seated in his regular seat which had become known as the Throne chair, and people quickly gathered around him. As fate would have it, there was a very socially prominent couple from Newport in the audience, and they were absolutely thrilled over the experience of meeting Sir John. By the end of the evening they were the best of buddies and promptly invited LADY CAROL, Sir John, my singer and myself, to their daughter's wedding which was to take place in two weeks. They would send a private jet to pick us up for the wedding, and assured us that it would be the social event of the year in Newport Beach. One thing was obvious. It did not take Sir John long to charm anyone he wanted to. The entire evening was fascinating to behold as people presented themselves to Sir John as if he were the Pope, and the only thing missing was the ritual of kissing the ring on the Pope's finger.

The following morning the thing that I remember most was that it had gotten a little drunk-out the night before. Feeling slightly hung over, I showered and shaved quickly. I was running late and it was past my normal seven a.m. arrival at the Inn. As I drove through the gates, I caught a glimpse of Sir John in his bathing suit, jogging back to his villa. THIS MAN WOULD NEVER CEASE TO AMAZE ME. How at 72 he could sit up that late, drink all night and still get up at 6 o'clock in the morning was beyond me.

It was about 10 o'clock a.m. when I was summoned to the courtyard area of the hotel to witness the local pet store stocking my pond with the most magnificent fish I have ever seen. Sir John was right there supervising to make sure that everything was perfect. It was the most breathtaking array of exotic fish I have ever seen in one place before. I did not know what to say, I was speechless. I was so full of gratitude I wanted to kiss him. We then went to his villa to supervise the installation of the one-hundred-gallon aquarium he had purchased for his living room. He invited me down to take a look at it, which I did out of curiousity more than anything else. As I approached this villa, I was stunned to see seven different bird cages hanging in the front patio with various types of birds. As I walked inside, I was overwhelmed at how beautiful the aquarium looked in the living room. At this point I must tell you that I had not been in Sir John's villa since he occupied it, and he had really changed it around to suit his taste right down to the fact he had a large chair that I had never seen before, in the middle of the living room and low chairs around it as if he were conducting court. What really surprised me was, as I looked around the room, I noticed many pieces of antique furniture and artifacts that had been *missing* from the hotel that I had been quite upset about. I did not have the nerve to ask Sir John where he had obtained these articles, or how he had come by them, as I figured out that the blessings of Sir John's presence far outweighed such trivia as was crossing my mind at that time. He then took me into the bedroom, where he showed me his magnificent crown on a red velvet pillow, which supposedly was the award for his Arabian horses. Scattered carelessly over the dresser, I noticed many large pieces of turquoise jewelry. Not knowing anything about jewelry and especially turquoise, I was always impressed at what appeared to be the many different magnificent pieces that Sir John wore daily. I never saw the same pieces twice. Sir John then excused himself as he pointed out he had a luncheon date with someone in the restaurant and had to get ready.

At about one o'clock, as I was strolling around the dining room, I noticed Sir John sitting with a woman whom I judged to be between 35–40. Sir John beckoned me over. He introduced me to Miss Jorgenson. She had a very deep, resonant voice which was out of character with her looks. Sir John was quick to point out that this was *the* Christine Jorgenson who had received the wide publicity as the first human being to have a sex-change operation. Sir John would never cease to amaze me.

That evening in the Lounge at about 9:30, lo and behold the door opened and there was Sir John *in a red velvet robe with a crown on his head.* I couldn't believe my eyes!! Everyone in the Lounge turned around and stared, and then broke out in a loud, cheering applause. Sir John explained that every once in a while he enjoyed his robe and crown, as it reminded him of the knighthood he had received from the Queen. It didn't really matter whether this man was real or not, he certainly was the most color-ful, flamboyant character I had ever met or even heard of.

The following day word had spread around Palm Springs about Sir John and his robe and crown, and there were even more people visiting the Ingleside Inn in the hopes of getting a glimpse of Sir John. It was about two days after that incident that we could not find our gar-dener. Now the gardener was thirty-two years old, a skinny man weighing approximately 130 lbs. with long, hippy-type hair, a beard, and needless to say, absolutely filthy looking. We had called his home for several hours, no answer. It was unlike him not to appear punctually every morning. Every-one was wondering where he was, when our Head House-keeper reported that if we were looking for Roger, the gardener, he was asleep in Sir John's villa *IN HIS BED.* Alarmed that I might scare off the best guest I would ever have, I ran down immediately to Sir John's villa, to find Sir John sitting on his front porch having a cup of tea, and playing with his birds. I started to apologize profusely about the gardener, when Sir John told me that Roger was there by his invitation as he appeared to be tired. Roger had been out the night before, and Sir John told him it was quite alright to take a nap in his bed.

Over the next few weeks at various times we found our dishwasher, bellmen, gardener and everyone else either sleeping, hanging around, "or smoking grass" in Sir John's villa. I really wasn't quite sure how to approach the situation as they were there by the invitation of Sir John himself. When I admonished one of the staff for visiting Sir John's villa, Sir John promptly called me on the carpet and said he had a right to invite whomever he wanted to his villa, as he was paying for it. At this point, I was not about to upset the apple cart and was willing to concede anything to Sir John.

The next day was the day of the wedding in Newport, and my schedule was too hectic to permit me to go. The private plane had arrived at Palm Springs Airport to pick up Sir John, my singer and Lady Carol. I must tell you they were a good-looking trio as they boarded the private jet for the big event. They returned that evening at about 8 o'clock with glowing reports of the lovely and impressive people that had attended the affair, and how well they had been treated. To deviate for a moment, all the pictures I eventually saw of the wedding, of which there were many, very few showed the bride and groom, but rather the newspapers emphasized the fact that visiting royalty had attended, mainly Sir John, Lady Carol, and George Allardice from Palm Springs.

During the course of the next few weeks, the season opened up in Palm Springs and Sir John was the most sought-after guest in the city. As a general rule, I don't attend many parties, but the few I did go to, Sir John was there in all his glory, and always the center of a crowd of people. His announcement that he was a permanent resident of the Ingleside Inn was a two-way street, as it added prestige to the Inn and at the same time gave Sir John credibility. Anyone who can afford to stay in a $160-a-day villa on an indefinite basis certainly had to be substantial.

Two months passed with Sir John rather prominent on the local hotel and restaurant scene. By this time he knew almost everyone in town. Poor Colonel Russ Hopf was still chasing him to close the deal on the two Rolls Royces, however, every day Sir John managed to string him out a little longer. His secretary was with him constantly, and his chauffeur spent every day washing the two cars, being Sir John's valet, and generally making himself available to anyone who needed help. It was not unusual for Sir John to loan out one of Colonel Hopf's Rolls Royces along with his chauffeur, and he quickly became the best-liked person in town. In order to keep himself occupied, he had announced that he would entertain the idea of buying a million-dollar home, and subsequently every real estate broker in town was romancing Sir John. Many of his days were spent in the back of a real estate limousine, being chauffeured and personally escorted through some of the best homes in Palm Springs.

To my knowledge, Sir John never had any intention of buying a home, but just thought it was an interesting way to spend his time.

Sir John mentioned one day that he would have to make a business trip to New Mexico to take care of some affairs regarding his turquoise mines. It was at that time I had some mechanics building some special dune buggies for me, and was having difficulty registering them with the Department of Motor Vehicles in California. Sir John suggested that I jot down the serial numbers of the engines and because the Governor of New Mexico was his friend, he would bring me back New Mexico registrations and license plates for the cars. He said it would then be easy to transfer them to California registration. I had nothing to lose, so I jotted down three different serial numbers on a piece of scratch paper with no legal documentation whatsoever, and gave them to Sir John. He returned approximately eight days later and lo and behold, he had three *New Mexico registrations*, and *three sets of license plates*. I couldn't believe it. There were many nights that I wondered about Sir John and I would always come to the same conclusion. Whatever game he was playing, I did not see any harm in it as he was not hurting anyone. I was reasonably sure that Sir John was a hoax, but nonetheless his bill was fairly current, and to my knowledge he had not asked anyone for anything. The only possibilities running through my mind were...perhaps he was living out a fantasy with a few dollars he had accumulated, and was going to spend them all in a few months in Palm Springs playing NUMERO UNO...perhaps he was setting up a ruse to win the confidence of some wealthy people and then con them... or perhaps the game was to meet and marry, or get money from some rich lady. On occasion, he escorted some of the best ladies around town, but he did not seem to diligently pursue that path.

Part of Sir John's story was that he had produced several pictures in Hollywood, and any names and facts he mentioned were always accurate to my knowledge. At one point he had stored some very valuable movie camera equipment in the hotel safe, and even though up to that point I had no reason to distrust Sir John, I was never really worried about my bill because I always had the camera and equipment in my safe, as collateral, which I knew were worth a few thousand dollars.

In my past business life, one of my investments had been a company who manufactured a unique line of belt buckles, and we were in the process of liquidating the company. Sir John claimed to be able to liquidate these belt buckles at about $1.50 apiece, and I had an inventory in the basement of about 3000 pieces. I knew sooner or later that Sir John's bubble would have to burst but I was not sure how it would come about, or what exactly would take place.

Sir John mentioned that he would be planning a trip to New Mexico in about two weeks and that he would take the belt buckles with him and would sell them. In the interim, Sir John was becoming even more prominent in town, and approximately two days before his scheduled trip the local newspaper devoted the entire second page of its edition to Sir John, with the title of "Royalty Invades the Desert." It was a very impressive interview.

Two days later, Sir John was planning to leave and mentioned that he had to take the camera equipment back to New Mexico, and he gave me some story as to why. I quickly checked his hotel bill and found it was the largest balance since he started staying with me, approximately $4200. He was going to take the only security I had (the valuable camera equipment), the $4200 hotel bill would be open, and additionally he was going to take $3000 worth of belt buckles with him because allegedly he had them sold. I had an ominous feeling that *this* was it. The circumstances seemed right, but I did not know how to confront him about it. If anything was going to happen, it would happen now. That night in the restaurant, Sir John approached me and said, "Please take care of my two Rolls Royces while I am gone." Now I was really stuck, as I knew the cars were not his. This would be the first time he would be gone when I would be left with no security.

Just then I received a phone call from a singer in Los Angeles who I had met in my restaurant, and with whom I had become very friendly. She called to invite Sir John and myself to the opening of a nightclub in Los Angeles, and said she would be most honored if both I and Sir John could attend. It was impossible for me as it was going to be a very busy night in the restaurant, but I conveyed the message to Sir John who was absolutely delighted and flattered and said that he could postpone his trip to New Mexico to attend the opening. He begged me to go with him, but I excused myself on the pretext of business. He then lined up two or three other people in town with whom he had become friendly, and they planned a big night in Beverly Hills for the opening.

The entourage left for Los Angeles at approximately 5 o'clock in the evening. At 6 o'clock that evening, Palm Springs Police came into the restaurant with a warrant for the arrest of Sir John. When I questioned them what it was about, they told me it was a bad check charge from Michigan. I explained to them that he had gone out of town and was expected to return the following morning. The word that there was a warrant out for the arrest of Sir John spread through Palm Springs like wildfire. At approximately 8 p.m., that evening, Sir John called me from Los Angeles as he had heard the police were looking for him and he wanted to know what it was all about. When I explained it to him, he said there must be some mistake. He asked if I could please find out more about it, and he would call me back in an hour. I checked with the Palm Springs Police who advised me they were going to stake out his room, and should he call back I was to keep him on the line so they could trace the call. In one hour I received the call in the Lounge. In the meantime, the police had taken over his villa, had closed off access to anyone and had set up a system whereby they could trace his call. I immediately sent a waiter to tell them I had Sir John on the phone. I stalled Sir John on the phone in the Lounge for several minutes. I explained to him that there was so much noise in the Lounge I could not hear him clearly, and asked him to please hold on while I went to the front of the Lounge. Then I told him something had come up in the restaurant, could he please hold on another minute. I then went to the men's room, washed my hands, dilly-dallied, came back. He was still on the phone and I spoke to him for another five minutes stalling for the police. He explained the bad check had to be a mistake. He kept repeating that there had to be some mistake, and that he would be back in the morning to clear up the whole matter. I hung up the phone and ran to Sir John's villa to see if the police had tracked the phone call. THEY TOLD ME I HAD NOT KEPT HIM ON THE PHONE LONG ENOUGH. I couldn't believe it. At that moment, there was a knock on the door of the villa, I opened it and saw Tony, Sir John's driver, standing there. He told me he had come to pack Sir John's belongings for the trip to New Mexico. The police immediately brought him in and started to question him about Sir John. It didn't take Tony long to break down, and he explained that approximately one week before showing up at the Ingleside Inn he was hitch-hiking when Sir John picked him up and told him he was going to be his personal valet, that he was not to say anything, but to go along with whatever he, Sir John said, and to play the role. Tony said he didn't know anything about Sir John other than as a result of meeting him he was living pretty well.

Tony was driving Sir John's secretary's car, a 4-seater Mercedes, and staying with her, and she had just received a phone call from Sir John telling Tony to go over to the villa and pack everything. He was then to return to the secretary's apartment where Sir John would call him later, telling him where to meet him. The police went out and searched the secretary's car. In the trunk they found one television set from the hotel and Tony swore he had no idea how it got there.

The police decided to keep Tony in the villa so he could have no communication with Sir John. He was to spend the night in the villa and await Sir John's arrival the next day. Sir John called me several times during the evening to try and pump me for information as to what was going on, but I did not let on anything about Tony or that the police were waiting for him. Needless to say, the next day came and went and Sir John never appeared.

There is a law to protect innkeepers, the Innkeepers Protection Law, which gives an innkeeper the right to impound any possessions of a guest until his bill is paid. The police carefully pointed out to me that everything in that villa belonged to me until I got paid.

The following day the police told me I should take everything in the villa and lock it in my safe until further developments. They went through all of Sir John's personal possessions and I do not know what they found. The following morning when I was in my office around 7 a.m., one of the bellmen ran up to me and said, "Somebody is removing something from Sir John's villa." Quickly I rushed down there and found the detective who had spent the night there, moving the aquarium. I called him over and said nothing could be removed from there until I was paid. The detective called me aside, said he was embarrassed, and wanted to talk to me privately. He said he did not know how to tell me this, but he owned the pet store from where Sir John had bought the aquarium. He had extended credit to Sir John for the aquarium, in addition to the fish in my pond, and had never been paid. He was taking the aquarium back in order to recoup some of his loss. He was totally embarrassed about the whole situation. What could I say? Sir John had conned the detective as well as everyone else.

While moving Sir John's belongings to my safe, we discovered 20 pairs of new shoes, maybe 50 garments, plus oodles of jewelry as well as a couple of velvet robes and all sorts of odd things. Sir John had worked up such confidence that the people he came in contact with trusted him implicitly, and had entrusted him with many valuable possessions.

The following day, Sir John called me and again reassured me that it was all a dastardly mistake and would I please ship his belongings to a certain address. I explained to him that I could not until I was paid, that I was sorry to have to take that position, but under the circumstances I had no choice. He tried every angle to coerce me into sending certain items to him. He said there was one attache case in which he had some very valuable jewelry plus extremely important papers, and would I please make sure to take good care of it until he straightened out this whole situation. I assured him it was in good, safe hands, and that I would take care of it pending the outcome of the whole mess.

Sir John's secretary then called me and asked if she could see me immediately, as it was urgent. I met her in the restaurant and she proceeded to tell me she had only met Sir John two months before he came to the Ingleside Inn. He had managed to persuade her that he was for real and had conned her out of $20,000 for some sort of investment. It seems for some reason she had also given him her jewelry, which was all she had left in the world, and could I please give this back to her, as now that her money was gone she was penniless. She knew the $20,000 was gone. When I asked her why she had played the role of secretary and lied for a man who was beating her out of money, she explained that at that point it was too late, the money was gone and the best she could do was to play along with Sir John in the hopes that by some miracle he could recoup some of the money and pay her back. She really had no choice, she said. I could not very well give away Sir John's belongings. However, with the police's blessing and a letter from the lady's lawyer, I allowed her to go through the several jewelry cases and pick out four pieces that belonged to her.

The next phone call I got was from a local singer in town whom I had met several times. She said she had to talk to me, and I invited her over for a cup of coffee. The act she did was modeled after Sophie Tucker's act. She told me she had spent her entire life savings to buy two velvet robes from Sophie Tucker, as she was a great fan of hers, and in doing her "Sophie Tucker" act she used them constantly. She had run into Sir John and he had convinced her to lend him the robes for some fun and games. She knew I had the right to keep them in my possession until I was paid, but they were hers and they represented not only a lot of money, but were of great sentimental value to her, and would I please be kind enough to give them back to her. There was no way I could deny this impassioned plea, so I dug them out of the safe and gave them to her.

At that time I had a little 70-year-old cashier working in the kitchen. She came to me with tears in her eyes and explained that she had given Sir John her three diamond rings she had accumulated over the 70 years of her life. Sir John was supposed to have had them appraised and tell her what they were worth. She asked me if I had noticed them amongst Sir John's belongings. When I told her I had, she begged me to give them to her as they were all she had in the world. Needless to say, I returned the three rings to the little lady.

I started then to receive more phone calls from people all over town all concerned about money that was owed to them by Sir John, and at that point I made a deal with the Palm Springs Police so that all the phone calls would be referred to them.

Three days passed and not a word was heard from Sir John. Early in the morning of the fourth day, I was calling one of the people who had gone to Beverly Hills with Sir John for the singer's opening. As soon as the voice on the other end of the phone answered, I knew at once it was SIR JOHN! I asked if Steve was there, playing dumb as if I had not recognized Sir John's voice, but he immediately recognized mine, disguised his voice and said Steve was not home. I left a message to have Steve call me when he returned, then advised the Police Department at once where Sir John was located. Two hours later the word was all over town that Sir John had a long criminal record, and according to the papers, he was a house painter in 1916 back in Detroit. The publicity was priceless. The formal charges were Grand Larceny and Forgery in New York State, and issuing worthless checks in New Mexico. They listed eleven aliases and a record stretching from 1938, including conviction for embezzlement, unarmed robbery and possession of an automatic weapon. According to Suffolk County Police in New York, Sir John was an Easthampton contractor and house painter, who was indicted in November 1972 after he stole a friend's car and sold it for $1500, forging his friend's name on the transfer. He served time in jail on various occasions. He had been arrested a dozen or so times, beginning in 1938. He was arrested for vagrancy in Florida in 1938; embezzlement in Michigan in 1947; stolen property in 1951 for which he spent time in the Federal Penitentiary in Pennsylvania. He was arrested again in Michigan in 1954; for malicious attempt to extort in Sioux City, Iowa in 1959; concealed weapon in New York in 1971, where again he served time in the Federal Penitentiary.

When Sir John was arrested, he immediately took an overdose of tranquilizers, and they had to pump his stomach. The irony of the whole story is that many local merchants visited him in the hospital, still convinced that there had been a mistake and that Sir John was really what they wanted him to be.

Two months after the incident a local attorney was hired on behalf of Sir John to pay my hotel bill and retrieve his possessions from my safe. In browsing through some of his paperwork, we found many pieces of correspondence from people with whom he had spent time in jail. We also found a check made on the Sir John Beech account to Universal Studios for $250,000. He had a collection of WHO'S WHO books from the movie industry, the social world, and the political world.

Sir John was a student of the wealthy and the affluent, and really had studied his facts and figures to pull off the pretense that he hobnobbed and traveled with these people. He actually worked hard at his craft. He did it well.

This story is written some years after the incident, and I must tell you in all sincerity that I, as well as everyone else who had come in contact with Sir John, had only fond memories of him and in spite of everything, truly enjoyed what I am sure will be one of the most interesting experiences and unforgettable characters we shall ever meet in all of our lives.

THE END

FREE LUNCH

NUMBER THREE
IN A SERIES
OF ONE MILLION

As usual, I appeared at my restaurant at 7:45 p.m., to do my nightly stint of chatting and smiling at customers. As soon as I entered the door, my Maitre d' informed me that there was a man at the bar who wanted to say 'hello.' The MD mentioned that this man was *very important!* He owned two race tracks, was very well-known, and the Maitre d' inferred he knew him personally. The Maitre d' was an inveterate horse player (which seems to be an occupational prerequisite in the restaurant industry), and knew all the horse owners, jockeys, and trainers, who came into the restaurant.

My Maitre d' brought me over to this man sitting at the end of the bar. He was about 55 years old, 5'6", 150 lbs., with a ruddy complexion, and he was wearing a Western tie and boots. I was then introduced to Mr. Tony Alessio, and he informed me that he owned Agua Caliente Race Track in Tijuana, and Ruidosa Downs in New Mexico. Mr. Alessio immediately asked me if I knew who he was, and, of course, I assured him I did. He called me aside and told me he had been with Frank Sinatra the day before in New York (where Sinatra was filming "Contract on Cherry Street"), and that Mr. Sinatra insisted he should make it his business to come in and say 'hello' to me. Having met Sinatra on several occasions, when he was a customer of my restaurant, I was very flattered and impressed. This man could have anything he wanted. He explained that Mr. Sinatra was flying in from New York Wednesday for some business, and that they would be having lunch at my restaurant. He requested I arrange for a secluded table for Sinatra, Spiro Agnew and himself (this was Monday), as he was thinking of using Mr. Agnew for publicity for his race tracks. I spent the next few minutes assuring Mr. Alessio that they would have total privacy at a secluded table where they would not be overheard, and that I would attend to the arrangement *personally*. He then said "Frank told me that you were good people and I am going to do something *for you*." (By this time I was forbidden to call him anything but 'Tony.')

He proceeded to tell me who he was, how big he was, and that his family was recently written up in Newsweek Magazine, and that he would bring in the article which was outside in his car. He went on to tell me about his brother, who was the subject of the Newsweek article, and in prison for income tax evasion. I was really impressed when he told me that his family was the subject of a book (which he would give me) and was actually a dynasty going back several hundreds of years, and having vast holdings in real estate, banking, etc., both in San Diego and Mexico.

Assuming that I was well-known and a "Connected Guy" (an expression to describe people who knew gangsters), he dropped every name I ever heard, and then some. Not wanting to confess that I was not as worldly as he might think, I greeted each name with a roar, smiling knowledgeably, and picked every third name to ask "How the hell is Joe Pineapple?" Some of these names actually sounded familiar from younger days when I read "Crime Does Not Pay" comic books.

At that point I recognized a Damon Runyan-type character (who was a jeweler) being seated in the restaurant. This gentleman never ceased to amaze me as he could pull out $75,000 worth of diamonds from his pockets at any given moment to show his customers. The jeweler also seemed to be very well-known, and always ran into people he knew in my restaurant. He had a thick European accent, and to hear him tell it, he sold diamonds to every big name in the world. His office was his pocket. I am not quite sure how big an office it was, but as I said before, what came out of there never ceased to amaze me. I excused myself from Tony to walk over and greet the jeweler. He invited me to have a drink, which I graciously accepted. We chatted awhile, and just to impress him I casually mentioned that I had the famous "Tony Alessio" at the bar. The jeweler said he knew Tony's brother very well because he often visited a friend of his in a *little-known* jail where Tony's brother was. I told him when the opportunity presented itself, I would introduce him.

I called the Maitre d' over to tell him I would like to introduce the jeweler to Mr. Alessio. The Maitre d' knew the jeweler from the days he worked at the Scandia Restaurant in Los Angeles, and they both started discussing how important the Alessio family was. The Maitre d' mentioned in conversation that one of my Mexican waiters had won several thousand dollars on a long shot daily double at the track at Agua Caliente only a couple of months before. Having the story as an excuse to reengage Tony in conversation at the bar, I wandered back into where he was sitting. I told the daily double story to Tony just to let him know I knew everything. He acknowledged he also knew about it. He said he had a "boat" race ("fixed" in street jargon) set up at Ruidosa Downs, and was going to cut me in for a piece of the "candy" (easy money). He would give me the name of the horse later. I had heard many stories of opportunities like this, but had never had the occasion to capitalize on one.

Just at that moment, my lady came in and joined me. I was all excited to show off my new-found and illustrious friend. What I love about this business is in the two short years I had been in it, at this time, I had made the acquaintance of many notables, celebrities, VIPs and accomplished people. "Tony" was one more feather in my cap. I introduced my lady to Tony and mentioned that Tony and I had many important mutual acquaintances.

During the conversation it came up that my lady was from Detroit, and Tony started to mention every wise guy from "Frankie Shotgun" to "Willie the Knife." As fate would have it, my gal had either heard the names before, went to school with one of their relatives, or through mutual friends had met them (not to imply that my lady was in that kind of a crowd, but as you often find, large cities are really small cities when it comes to knowing everyone).

Please understand, basically I was "high" on the fact that Frank Sinatra had insisted this man should come in to say 'hello', and that obviously he was a "heavy hitter." (A favorite expression of mine to describe important people.) The fact that I was now going to share in a financial windfall "was just icing on the cake" for another great evening at Melvyn's Restaurant and Lounge.

As we were all having a swell time, a young lady approached me to ask if I were the owner. She said she and her girlfriend had been invited down by some gentlemen to attend a charity event that Frank Sinatra was headlining, and she had forgotten where it was and could I help her. Embarrassed not to know about such an important event, I turned to Tony at the bar, and asked him if he knew anything about it. He said sure, that it was Wednesday night at the Riviera Hotel, and that was why he had made reservations for luncheon on that same day. It was a personal charity of Frank Sinatra's, and that was why he was flying into town on Wednesday from New York. Seeing how disappointed the girls were that they had the wrong day, Tony immediately bought them a drink. I then left the two ladies, my girl and Tony to chat, while I did one "nightly" tour of the dining room. The two girls had already left and Tony was sitting alone with my gal at the bar when I returned. By this time Tony seemed a little high, and he called me aside to tell me the name of the horse was Diamond Girl in the 6th race, and that I would make a lot of money as the horse was 20-1. Now I have received many tips in my life but never one from the owner of a race track, especially one in "McGoonsville" where you could probably pull anything you wanted. In spite of the above, I am a big boy and not too many people in my life have *handed me money*. I asked Tony how much I should bet and he, of course, said everything I could. He explained that bookmakers didn't handle such a small track, but he was flying back the following day and would place the bet for me. He made me swear not to mention this to anybody. He said that when he came in Wednesday for lunch and handed me an envelope full of money, I should just take it and not say a word. My heart started to palpitate as I considered the possibilities while the calculator in my brain worked at full speed. At no time did I consider the amount I might lose, but only how much I wanted to be in that envelope on Wednesday. For some reasons I figured $6,000 as the right number.

Sport that I am, I ripped out three $100 bills and said "here." (Five years before I would have begged, borrowed and stolen to bet as much as I could, but based on all the *great* tips over the past years, I guess I was a little gun-shy.) Tony looked at me and laughed. He said he was betting $100 for the Maitre d' AS A TIP! He belittled me sufficiently for me to rip out another two $100 bills. He was still reluctant to accept such a menial wager, but he finally condescended, after I jokingly said it didn't matter how much I won as I would probably give it to my girlfriend anyway. Just as I was handing him the money, a local bartender from another hotel came in with his wife. Tony mentioned he was waiting for them and all three went to sit in the Lounge. *Of course*, I sent over a drink *immediately*, and then took my girlfriend into the dining room to join the jeweler's table. I told the jeweler the story that Tony had just handed me $10,000 (20-1 on a $500 bet) and asked the jeweler if things like that really happened? He asked me if I would feel better if he verified Tony's authenticity. I said *absolutely*, and then called the Maitre d' over and asked him to find an excuse to introduce my jeweler friend to the "illustrious Mr. Tony Alessio!" The introduction was made in the Lounge. They discussed the little-known jail, the jeweler's friend who Tony knew, Tony's brother and various other things. The jeweler came back to the tables and said, "He's real." The jeweler returned to the table and pulled out two $100 bills and said—"Here, I want part of your action."

The Maitre d' walked over to the table and said "Mr. Alessio just bawled me out and said, 'Don't ever introduce me to anybody without my okay.' " (Spoken like a true big shot, I thought, and I was really impressed.) I then explained to my Maitre d' what had transpired and asked him how much of the bet he wanted. He told me Mr. Alessio was already betting $100 for him, and he would take $50 more. I went crazy and said "You are the horse player. How can you bet $50 on the horse and me $450. (I didn't tell him the jeweler took $200 of my bet.) YOU PLAY THE HORSES, I DON'T AND YOU PERSONALLY KNOW THIS GUY!" I then told the Maitre d' he had $100 on the horse — *he had no choice*. So far I was doing better than I ever had before. I bet $500 and already had $300 back.

Just then a good friend of mine walked in — Marc Lawrence. Marc is a very well-known character actor, and has played the "heavy" in 200 or more movies. *Everybody* knows his *face* but few know his name. Marc's favorite pastime is sitting at the bar and "goofing" on some of the "fabulous characters" that come in. In the short period of time I have known Marc, I have come to consider him a good friend and confidant. Knowing that this new character I had met was right up his alley, I started to tell Marc the story. I wanted to impress Marc that I knew people of Mr. Alessio's stature. I was anxious to show Tony that well-known people like Marc were in my immediate circle of friends. At this time, the couple Tony had been sitting with left, and he returned to the bar by himself. I told Tony I wanted to introduce him to my friend Marc, and he was agreeable. They quickly took to each other and really cemented their relationship when they discovered that both knew Lucky Luciano. (If only my friends in Brooklyn could see me now. There were *no big names* that were not part of my new world. If I say so myself, I have taken the whole "trip" pretty much in my stride. My hat size was only increased 3″!)

After I made the introduction, I wandered over to some other guests at the bar. One gentleman, a regular, nightly two-drink customer, was at the bar and I went over to chat with him. The jeweler came over to say 'goodbye' and kiddingly I told him to send an armored car around Wednesday to pick up his winnings. He told me he had plenty of room in his "office" (his pockets).

Marc and Tony meanwhile were having a ball in the bar reminiscing about all the people they knew. I overheard names like Lucky Luciano, Frank Sinatra, Al Capone, plus many other assorted characters they were discussing. As fate would have it, my regular customer with whom I was sitting was a personal friend of Mr. Sinatra's, and questioned me about the guy at the end of the bar who was dropping names so loudly. Excitedly, I told him the story, and he expressed doubt that Mr. Sinatra was going to be in town, and that he had not heard about it, although he admitted it was possible. As he was probably the most negative guy I have ever met, I took his comments in stride. He then suggested that I call someone we both knew who was really close to Frank. I called the other man to find out if Frank was expected to town, and he also said he knew nothing about the charity event, but suggested I call the Riviera Hotel to find out if it was on the schedule that week. This sounded like a good idea, so I called the Riviera Hotel who said they knew nothing about the affair. I insisted there must be some mistake. I finally called the owner of the hotel at home and it took him to convince me there was no such event scheduled.

I was a little confused at this point. I drifted over to Marc and Tony (they were getting along famously), and casually asked Tony if he was sure this charity event was this Wednesday. He seemed a little perturbed that I interrupted his new-found "love affair," and assured me it was. Now, even more confused I returned to my negative friend, Herb, and told him what had transpired. He then suggested I find out where Alessio was staying. In order to get into the conversation with Tony and Marc, I strained my memory for gangsters out of the past so I could join in. When I came up with "Louie the Lip," I was welcome to join in the "nostalgia game." Knowing the answer even before I slipped the question about where Tony was staying, he looked at me surprised at my naivete, and said "I am staying at Frank's, of course!" I now returned to Herb to figure out the next step of my investigation. I must admit that at this point, I myself was getting a little dubious, mainly because the names he was mentioning are not usually repeated loudly in public. (In my experience, people in that type of circle never drop names, and if they do, they whisper them very discreetly.)

Herb then told me he had seen Tony paying a check for a $1.50 beer with a hundred dollar bill. It quickly dawned on me it must have been one of the five I had given him. I ran into the dining room and found the Maitre d', and called him into a secret huddle. "Are you sure this guy's Tony Alessio?" I asked him. He replied, "Before you came in, we chatted awhile and he seems to know all about the race tracks, horses, and all other things, plus you had the jeweler verify him. Why would he try and fool you?"

Really confused at this point, I figured out the best thing I could do would be to have Marc Lawrence verify Tony's authenticity. I ran to an in-house telephone at the back of the Lounge and had my friend, Marc, paged to the phone so I could tell him of my suspicions. I explained my fears to Marc, urging him to test and verify Tony, and briefly explained what had transpired to the last few minutes. Just as I was about to hang up, who comes sauntering over to me but good old Tony Alessio. "Mel, I just wanted to say 'goodnight' and make sure everything is all set for Wednesday." At that point I almost swallowed the phone. I thanked him profusely, and assured him I could not wait to see him again. (What an understatement!) As he started to walk out of the Lounge, I quickly called the parking lot attendant to take the license plate number of his (Tony's) car. Two minutes later the attendant called me back to say Tony had not called for any car but was WALKING OFF THE PROPERTY. I ran out into the street just as Tony was pulling away in a PICK-UP TRUCK! I didn't know whether to laugh or to cry. I went back to the bar, found Marc and reviewed the whole evening. We put our heads together and figured out the horse was not a 20-1 long shot, but that Tony Alessio was.

I must explain here that I have been "conned" 472 times in my life and for much greater sums of money, but I must admit, I was getting a little tired of this nonsense.

I could not sleep that night as my mind was going a mile a minute reviewing everything that had taken place. I could not wait for morning so that I could start to verify all the questions that were spinning in my mind. For some reason, I clung to the weakest explanation as being the most significant. (I just couldn't believe that anyone in Palm Springs would have the nerve to throw Frank Sinatra's name around, as this is a very small town.)

The following morning I called Ruidosa Downs to find out THEY WERE NOT OPEN FOR TWO MORE MONTHS. Still hoping against hope, I figured he meant Agua Caliente Race Tack, and that I had misunderstood him. I called my Maitre d', woke him up and told him to come right over to the restaurant. He was incredulous when I told him the story, and felt that the confusion was in my mind and that Wednesday WE WOULD BOTH BE RICH. Then we figured out that our next move would be to contact the local bartender who was having drinks with Tony Alessio the night before and find out what he knew. After ten phone calls to track him down, he said that he knew this man as Tony Alessio through a customer of his from San Diego. He told me this customer usually had lunch at the place he worked every day at 12:30. Not knowing what else to do at this point, I anxiously awaited the lunch hour so I could find this fellow from San Diego who knew Tony Alessio. I got to the bartender's place about 12 o'clock to make sure I didn't miss the guy. The bartender told me that *HE* had just gone to get a cashier's check to bet on the horse. Mr. Alessio was expected to pick it up. Just then the man who originally introduced the bartender to Tony Alessio came into the restaurant and the bartender introduced me to him. I pounced on the poor guy and started questioning him about Alessio. He explained to me that he owned several restaurants in San Diego, and Tony Alessio had been coming into his place for the past six months and that as far as he knew, he was Tony Alessio.

At this point there was nothing more I could do, and I am still hoping against hope that it was my mistake and that I misunderstood Mr. Alessio.

We still have his private table set in the corner of Melvyn's in the hope that I did misunderstand and took the wrong date, week, month — or maybe the wrong year!

As Fate Would Have It

Number Four
In a Series
Of One Million

I had just opened Melvyn's Restaurant and Lounge at the posh Ingleside Inn a week before, and was somewhat in a state of euphoria because of the many VIPs, celebrities, and notables who had walked through my doors in that short period of time. I was informed by my Maitre d' that he had just taken a reservation for the publisher of the local newspaper, a Mr. Ted Grofer, who was coming with a party of four. Needless to say, I was most *anxious* to make a good impression with the head of the *most* important newspaper in Palm Springs. I told my Maitre d' that the minute his party was seated, to let me know so I could meet him.

I was sitting at the bar chatting with a customer when the Maitre d' motioned me over. He said, "I just seated the Grofer party at table 20." I pulled myself erect, straightened my jacket, checked myself in the mirror (I had used artificial face bronzer that night, and I was never going to look better than this), and walked over as confidently as I could. I walked up, stretched out my hand, KNOCKING OVER A BOTTLE OF WINE, and said, "It's my pleasure to meet you, Mr. Grofer," my facade of confidence immediately blown. I started at once to apologize profusely, and asked the guests if they would please move back from the table so I might switch the table with the one immediately next to them. The man sitting on the right of the gentleman whose hand I shook very casually said, "Number One, *I* am Mr. Grofer, and Number Two, don't you think it would be easier to change the tablecloth than the table?" I giggled nervously, and explained to him that this was evidence of my long and extensive background in the restaurant business of ONE WEEK. I knew I had accomplished part of my purpose, which was to make an impression. I am not quite sure that was the impression I had wanted to create, *but it was an impression nevertheless.* I was rescued by a message that I had a phone call just as I was contemplating how I could possibly get out of there. I had figured out if my future in the restaurant business was going to be anything like that, plus the other similar experiences of the past week, my best solution was to build a series of trap doors throughout the restaurant so I could exit gracefully.

Although my function at night is to circulate throughout the dining room with a big smile on my face, I managed to avoid passing the Grofer table. I was absolutely new to the business, and had no idea what it was I was supposed to do when I circulate. But in all the movies I have seen, the restaurant owner always circulates with a very knowledgeable look on his face, and I was grateful for the fact that little pieces of debris and lettuce fell on the floor during dinner, as my picking them up as I walked around seemed to justify my existence. On approximately my seventh tour of the dining room, about two hours after I had been to the Grofer table, he caught my attention and motioned me to come over to the table. He said, "Don't be embarrassed, these kind of things happen." He said that he and his party would like to go into the Lounge and hear the entertainment for a while, and asked if I could set them up with four seats. I said I would only be a minute, and promptly went back and managed to secure the four best seats in the Lounge for them. I escorted his party to the back of the Lounge personally. I was feeling a lot better about the situation. Not wanting to impose, I kept my distance and then decided to go back and see how they were enjoying everything. AS FATE WOULD HAVE IT, as I approached the back of the Lounge, the cocktail waitress slipped and a bottle of wine fell over the table at which they were sitting, and soaked the entire party. Being the "stand-up guy" that I was, I immediately turned on my heels and ran out the front of the restaurant. When I got outside, I realized I had NO PLACE TO GO, no place to hide, and sooner or later I would have to face the music. I sauntered back to the Grofer party and played stupid, as if I had not seen the accident. When I asked how everything was, the publisher's wife informed me what had happened, and said that the dress she was wearing was very expensive (her lack of compassion and understanding was only a small indication of the amount of her irritation). I offered to replace the dress, having no idea of what I might be getting into. Fortunately, she said she would settle for a good cleaning. I apologized profusely, thanked them for their understanding, and assured them I would make it up to them.

About one week later, Mr. Grofer called me on the phone personally, and said he and a group of important people he wanted to entertain and would like to have a reservation. He would like to bring them to Melvyn's, and would I, myself, look after the arrangements. Overwhelmed that I had a chance to make amends so quickly, I marked on the reservation sheet "GROFER VIP, party of 6 at 8:00." The reservation was for a Saturday night, which is always "total chaos" in Palm Springs. It is not unusual in any Palm Springs restaurant to wait a considerable time on a Saturday evening, *even though* you have reservations.

So many things were happening to me — I was meeting so many new people...the business was new to me and consequently I was always in a constant state of confusion. Being one of the world's greatest LIST MAKERS, things had gotten so bad that I was beginning to make notes to remind myself to take a shower and shave. By the time Saturday night came, I was in a terrible state of confusion and nervous about all the reservations we had. I arrived at the restaurant at 7:45 in the evening to find a crowded foyer of people waiting to be seated. Several different people grabbed me to tell me that they knew my Aunt Tillie back in Brooklyn, or that they had gone to school with my cousin, Shelley, etc. By the time I worked my way to the back of the Lounge, it was 9 o'clock. Who should be sitting there but Mr. Grofer with his party. He called me over and very facetiously said, "We have already been waiting one hour, how much longer do you think it will be?" The tone of his voice would have kept ice cream frozen; I could not believe I had forgotten. I had put it on my list but I forgot to make a note to look at my list. I ran back immediately to the Maitre d' and asked him what had happened, because I had marked the reservation "VIP." He informed me he did not understand my writing and he thought the name of the party was "G. Rofen VIP." It took about ten minutes before I was able to get Mr. Grofer and his party seated, and at this point, I figured the only article about me that would make the Desert Sun newspaper would be my "OBITUARY" or "BANKRUPTCY" notice, depending upon which came first. My manager, who was a veteran of thirty years in the business, told me not to take it so hard, and what I should do on Monday morning is to call Mr. Grofer personally and invite him with his wife to dinner at the restaurant as my guests. Taking heart at the possibility that this might be my salvation, I couldn't wait until Monday morning to "right my wrongs."

They say time is a great healer, and I sincerely believe it because when I reached Mr. Grofer Monday morning, the tone of his voice indicated that "fear is worse than fear itself." I told him that he would do me a great service if, at his convenience, he and his wife would give us another try and be my guests. He thanked me, said it was very nice of me, and he would see if he could coerce his wife into coming back. Now, usually I take off two weekday nights in order to recoup my strength and my sanity. I was off that Thursday night and when I came in Friday, my Maitre d' called me over and said he had to talk with me. He said, "Mr. Haber, I don't know how to tell you this, but I goofed with Mr. Grofer last night!!!" I couldn't believe it, and really didn't want to hear the story, but I had no choice. It seems that though I had invited him as my guest, I neglected to tell anybody, assuming that when he wanted to come in he would make the reservation with me personally. What happened was, he came in with his wife ON MY NIGHT OFF, had dinner, and as he was about to leave, he thanked the waiter and give him a tip. He then started to walk out. The waiter in his patriotic course of duty said, "Excuse me, Sir, BUT YOU HAVE NEGLECTED TO PAY THE CHECK." I gathered from that, that there was even more to it. Maybe he even "jumped" Mr. Grofer as if he were trying to beat the house! Having been confronted before several other customers, and rather embarrassed about the whole thing, it seems Mr. Grofer simply pulled out the money and paid the check. It was one of the few times in my life that I was capable of crying.

In order to console me, my manager explained that in this business every restaurant has what they call "jinxed customers." Not knowing what else to do, I sat down and composed one of the most apologetic letters in my "erring" life. I just about told him that to forgive is divine, and that should he ever have the nerve to risk coming into our restaurant again, I, personally, would be the doormat at the front door for him to walk on. I immediately set up a mental block about his name, and his newspaper, because the mere thought of it gave me cramps in my stomach.

Approximately a month later, on a Wednesday night, I walked into the restaurant and much to my surprise, sitting at a big center table, were six men and one of them was none other than Ted Grofer! I approached the table on tiptoes, and at this point, the whole situation was so outrageous that the first comments out of my mouth was "I can't believe you came in here without a helmet!" Mr. Grofer replied, "Mel, I think maybe making the reservation in my name is bad luck, so we made it in someone else's name, and I thought maybe we could get away with it without incidence." He went on to say there wasn't a chance in the world that his wife would come back, but that he ENJOYED LIVING DANGEROUSLY. Totally relieved I went into a comic routine for his whole party, explaining the "jinxed" customer routine, poking fun at myself and my lack of experience in the business, and a good time was had by all. By this time I was seated in the group and everybody was really getting off on me, primarily on my stupidity, inexperience, and all those good qualities that make a man successful. I must have been sitting there forty-five minutes telling my life story, of how I got into such an unlikely situation as the restaurant business, when Ted Grofer suggested a toast to the new host in town. With that, as he stood up to make the toast, the waiter was passing with a tray and — need I say it — Mr. Grofer's head hit the tray and four hot entrees spilled on the table. I am not quite sure whether he was serious or kidding when he picked up a knife and made manacing gestures towards me, but I didn't wait around to find out. I simply shrugged my shoulders, walked out the front door, got into my car and went home.

I know this story sounds unbelievable, but it is absolutely true. By this time the whole series of episodes was so outrageous and so unbelieveable that you can only laugh about it.

Another few months passed with Mr. Grofer nowhere in sight. On a weekday afternoon at lunchtime, lo and behold, there's Mr. Grofer sitting at the table with another gentleman. There is no way I was going to go anywhere near that table. As fate would have it, it was pouring rain (unusual for Palm Springs). I was hiding in the back of the restaurant when my manager came back and said to me, "You will not believe what has just happened!" It seems Mr. Grofer received an important phone call from his wife while he was having lunch. She told him that her car would not start and she had to pick up their son at school, and would he run over and pick up the child. He went out to get his car and discovered that by accident, when the parking lot attendant opened the door for him, the atten-dant inadvertently hit the automatic lock control of the doors and Mr. Grofer's car had been sitting there in the teeming rain, engine running, with all the doors locked. And exactly at that moment he went out, the car ran out of gas! As if that were not bad enough, his car was blocking the entrance to the restaurant, and they were driving the other customers' cars over my beautiful lawn in order to get the people out of the rain. I offered to drive him to pick up his son and he very wisely said "No thank you." Not to be discouraged by his refusal of my help, I insisted he take one of my twelve cars. He agreed, thanked me, and left.

Fifteen minutes later, my secretary informed me there was a Mr. Grofer on the phone. Pleased that he had enough courtesy to call and thank me, I picked up the phone and said "Hello Ted." In a voice that wreaked of murder, he slowly and carefully explained exactly where he was with A FLAT TIRE!

Over the following year I have run into Mr. and Mrs. Ted Grofer at many social events, and we were able to joke about it as they were no longer coming back to the restaurant, and therefore no harm could befall them. This was perfectly okay with me, because it was more important that I become their friend than they become my customers. He accepted the theory that this did not happen to everybody, and he was strictly a jinx at Melvyn's. At one private party we both attended, he finally broke down and said that both he and his wife thought I had the best atmosphere in town, absolutely loved the place, and that did I think there was a possibility that they could celebrate their anniversary WITHOUT ANY SERVICE CATASTROPHIES. I told him that my personal supervision was no longer enough, and that I would pray to the gods for their help.

The following Friday night as I watched their table carefully, I could not believe my good fortune. Everything seemed to be fine. I had made a deal with Mr. Grofer that I would not come over to the table until they were ready to leave. Just then, the "Melvyn's Boys Choir" (a group of waiters and bus boys used to sing for special occasions) started singing "Happy Birthday" at the table. IT WAS THEIR ANNIVERSARY! As they paid their check, they both let out a great sigh of relief, and were grinning from ear to ear as they motioned for me to come over. I stood at their table repeating over and over again, "I told you we could do it — I told you we could do it!" In my enthusiasm, while I was flapping my hand around to make my point more dramatic, you guessed it. I knocked the glass of water RIGHT IN MRS. GROFER'S LAP.

I have not seen the Grofers in the last six months. By coincidence, it is their son who is the newspaper boy for my home where I get the daily delivery of the local Desert

Sun. If they happen to read this story, I want them to know I am trying to make amends in my small way. Do you think a $20 tip per week to a 14-year-old newspaper delivery boy is excessive???

I FAILED MY MEMORY COURSE

NUMBER FIVE
IN A SERIES
OF ONE MILLION

Over that first summer, there were many locals who stopped by the Inn to see what was happening. The word was all over town that some "slick guy from New York" with plenty of money took it over, and I received lots of advice, opinions and comments. I put together my hotel crew during the month of September. My Front Desk consisted of a very nice-looking man about fifty years old; I had gotten him through a hotel agency in Los Angeles. He was an ex-alcoholic who obviously had gone astray, but was perfect for appearances sake. In addition, there were two other people for the Front Desk that I don't even remember now. I managed to get back the original, flower-picking housekeeper. I hired a 60-year-old veteran Bell Captain by the name of Luke, and kept Skip and Larry to work with him and do odd jobs. Jay was my aide-de-camp, and my hotel staff was set. I hired a local Maitre d' and he staffed the dining room.

September was drawing to a close, and the place was looking pretty good. We were not completely finished, but I had come to the realization that I would *never* be completely finished. Charlie, the chef, had put together a very ambitious menu. We decided to open the doors on the last Friday in September. I chose not to plan any big opening, but to sort of open quietly, so that I could iron out any kinks that existed. I placed a small ad in the local newspaper announcing that Melvyn's was now serving dinner. I had made up a critique sheet that I was going to use throughout the first week of operation, in order to get the customers' reactions. It was presented at every table with the check, and the waiter was instructed to buy a round of drinks for every table that filled it out.

As I was driving to the restaurant Opening Night, I had no idea what to expect. As I walked through the doors,

I was surprised to find the bar full of people and the dining room full. To say I was nervous is an understatement. The Maitre d' informed me we were sold out. Wow! I never would have guessed. As I looked around the totally unfamiliar crowd, it seemed that all the women were beautiful, all the men were great-looking, and that everybody was beautifully dressed. I had hassled with myself that day as to whether or not to wear a tie, but luckily had made the right decision to do so. Had I guessed wrong, I would have been totally out of place as all the men were wearing ties. The Maitre d' pulled me into a corner in the dining room and started to give me a run-down on the people who were there. As he related their names and who they were, I got all the more nervous. It sure seemed like I had the "Who's Who" of Palm Springs. I circulated throughout the dining room and bar for about two hours, having no idea what I actually should be doing. Several people stopped me and introduced themselves and wished me good luck. This was going to be more fun than I thought. I had hired a piano player for the Lounge and he was tinkling in the back, and that area started to fill up with customers. Over the summer, I had become friendly with a nice young man about nineteen who used to come around and offer any help he could. We had just taken a liking to one another. His name was Danny; he was a college student who supported himself by parking cars at a restaurant two blocks away. He had assured me that when I opened he would recommend people to my place.

That night, several people walked in and mentioned that Danny had sent them. About 10 o'clock, I walked outside to have a cigarette, and just at that moment, a motorcycle pulled up with a guy dressed in dungarees, a T-shirt and a beard, certainly not the Ingleside type. Seated behind him was a pretty girl. The guy said he had come to see the new place. Politely I told him it was opening night and would he please come back another time. He smiled at me and simply drove off. I was pleased with myself for handling the situation so adeptly. About 11:00 p.m., my young friend, Danny, showed up and said, "Mel, have you been getting all the people I sent?" I told him I had, and thanked him. He asked how I enjoyed meeting Steve McQueen and Ali McGraw. Startled and disappointed that I had not, I said they hadn't shown. He was surprised because they said they would go right over and have a drink with me. I told Danny I would have known if they had come in. He said, "They were on a big, blue Harley Davidson motorcycle, and Steve McQueen was wearing jeans and a T-shirt!" It was to be the first of many blunders.

One of the biggest assets you can have as a successful restaurateur is a great memory for names. Unfortunately, this is not one of my attributes, and there were three incidents that took place almost immediately that taught me you really can't bluff your way through.

The first one concerns one of the great names in motion picture history, who started frequenting my place right after it opened. He was the legendary Darryl Zanuck. I was very impressed that the legendary Mr. Zanuck had chosen my place as one of his favorites, and at that time he was dining in the restaurant regularly, three times a week. Of the many VIPs and celebrities that came in, I was most impressed by him, because he was at the pinnacle of power when I was a child and most impressionable. Also, I might add, at that point in time was Mr. Cecil B. DeMille, and their names to me were almost synonymous. It seemed that whenever I read about one, I read about the other. I often refer to the fact that I was twenty-eight years old before I discovered Ferrante and Teicher were two people, as I always thought it was one guy playing a hell of a piano.

It was probably the twentieth time Mr. Zanuck came into the restaurant when I walked up to him, extended my arm, and said, "Good evening, Mr. DeMille, how do you feel today?" Without blinking an eye, Mr. Zanuck muttered under his breath, "He's been dead ten years." I tried to pass it off as an intentional pun, but got nowhere, and it was just one of many embarrassments I was to suffer in my new-found career.

The second incident that sticks in my mind was during one very busy Saturday evening, when a woman whose name I should have known, having chatted with her several times, gave me a big greeting which I returned, avoiding, however, the use of her name. She inquired about my lady's well-being and I told her she would be staying at home that evening. She said, "Please give her my regards." I assured her I would, and went about my wandering. I passed her table again about ten minutes later, and she said, "Please make sure you tell Carol I was asking for her." Again I assured her I wouldn't forget. About an hour and a half later, after the lady had finished her dinner and was leaving the restaurant, she came by to bid me farewell, and for the third time, said, "Now don't forget to tell Carol I was asking for her," and again, I swore on all that was holy I would do it. She looked at me and said, "What is my name?" I stammered, stuttered, faked a coronary, and used every ploy to avoid the embarrassment, and now, years later, she has never forgotten to mention it. However, I have improved in this area considerably, as I actually do remember her name...about one-third of the time!

It was seven o'clock on a Saturday evening and I was showering and shaving at my home getting ready for a

Saturday night in the restaurant. Saturday nights in Palm Springs restaurants are unique unto themselves. It is basically a Saturday-night town, and you do about 60% of your business on that one evening. The phone rang, I answered it, and the voice on the other end of the line said, "Hello, Melvyn, this is Dave Matthews." I recognized the name immediately as being a very substantial and important man in Palm Springs, both socially and in business. I knew I liked him, but for the life of me I could not picture what he looked like. Dave went on to explain that he was embarrassed over the nature of the call and that he had never done this before. He was coming to dinner at my restaurant about eight o'clock with some very important people, and would I be kind enough to make a big fuss over him.

In the two short months I had been in the restaurant business, I'd discovered that as owner of the "In Chic" restaurant, people cultivated your attention and acquaintance. It was a phenomenon that I never quite understood, but I was thoroughly enjoying my new-found importance, nevertheless. There was no doubt that Dave was really uneasy and truly embarrassed. I suppose he felt it would make an impression on his important guests if I really did make a big to-do over him. My mind was racing a mile a minute, as I had no idea how to ask how I would recognize him. Considering the embarrassment he was already experiencing over asking me this favor, I would hate to add to it by asking him how I would recognize him. I'm sure that would be the ultimate blow to his ego. Anyway, I assured him it was no imposition at all, and that even without his special request, I considered him to be an important enough customer to go out of my way to show him special attention. Ingeniously I explained that it was always so chaotic on a Saturday night that just to make sure there were no slip-ups in the dark Lounge amidst masses of people, perhaps he should tell me what he would be wearing. I went on to explain that being new to the business plus the nervousness usually accompanying Saturday night, people tended to become faceless under those conditions. He said he would be wearing a navy blazer with a white open shirt and a white breast-hanky, and would be in a party of six arriving approximately at 8 o'clock.

Not taking any chances, at ten minutes to eight I stationed myself at the end of the bar right near the entrance to the restaurant. Almost to the second at 8 o'clock, the door opened and a party of six walked in; the first gentleman through the door was wearing a navy blazer, white open shirt, and white breast-hanky. Immediately I rushed over to him and said "Mr. Matthews, how great to see you, welcome back," and carried on as if he were God himself. Quickly the man standing *behind* the one I was addressing stepped up and in a tone that is difficult to describe said, "Melvyn, *I* am Mr. Matthews!"

What was he wearing? A navy blazer, with a white open shirt and a white breast-hanky, the same as the gentleman in front of them.

Suffice it to say that these stories taught me a lesson, and now my standard response is "Please forgive me, I have met so many people in such a short period of time, I know your face, but for the moment have forgotten your name."

The last story is, I think, a classic and one I love to tell. It seems that one of my regular customers had some friends visiting from Long Island in New York, and brought them to dinner at my restaurant. The people from New York loved it, and were very impressed. They returned to New York and when some neighbors mentioned they were planning a visit to Palm Springs, they told them to make *certain* that they ate at Melvyn's Restaurant, as it was the fashionable "in" spot, and would be an absolute must on their trip to Palm Springs. Ultimately I heard from the people who lived in Palm Springs that the couple came out from New York and stayed in one of the local hotels. They decided to eat out their first night at this great restaurant they had heard so much about. The only problem was, they had forgotten the name. However, they figured this would not present a difficulty as they remembered it was a man's name. They also felt certain that everyone would know the Number One fashionable restaurant in town that had a man's name. They got all dressed up with great anticipation of their dining experience. They got into a taxicab, explained to the driver they wanted to go to the best restaurant in town, and that it was named after a man.

They wound up having dinner at Elmer's Pancake House!

<u>LOVE AT FIRST</u> - ?

NUMBER SIX
IN A SERIES
OF ONE MILLION

There was a young guy in town who was a frequent customer at the restaurant. He was a regular type guy and often came with various different, but always pretty ladies. One of the more eligible bachelors, so to speak. He was about 37 years old, had been married once, made a reasonably good living, and had no problem enjoying a great social life.

One Saturday night he was seated in the back of the Lounge with a group of about six people. My girlfriend joined them, and they sat around having drinks and chatting for approximately two hours. I stopped by, chatted for a while, and was introduced to his date. My lady and I left the restaurant about midnight, after we said our goodnights, and went home.

Monday morning this guy called me up, all excited, and told me that after leaving my restaurant that evening, he had flown to Las Vegas and got married. Needless to say, I was very surprised, immediately called my girlfriend and told her that Arnie went and got married to Linda that night. She pointed out immediately that I had made a mistake in names, as the girl he was with was Vickie. It was not uncommon for me to make a mistake in names, so I thought nothing of it. About three or four hours later, Arnie called me back on some other business, and I asked him the name of the girl he married, and he said 'Linda.' Somewhat confused, I told him I had just spoken to my lady who told me he had been with Vickie. He said he was with Vickie, but he married Linda. He went on to explain that about twenty minutes after I left, a young lady came into the restaurant lounge with a guy. He started chatting with her while her date was getting drunk. They went out to the pool and had a drink, and after chatting for another hour they both realized they had found what each was looking for. He suggested they go immediately to Las Vegas to get married, and she agreed. They drove to a small airport in the area to find a plane to Las Vegas, only to find the airport closed and they finally wound up in Los Angeles where they took a regularly scheduled airplane. This really had to be one of the great love stories of all times, and as Arnie tells it on the way to the wedding chapel, which incidentally was appropriately named the "We've Only Just Begun Wedding Chapel," Arnie asked his bride-to-be "By the way, what is your last name?"

It wasn't until after they had already been married that Arnold discovered she didn't even live in Palm Springs, but in the Orange County area. At last sighting, they were both deliriously happy, and this story gave me a great inspiration to promote a cocktail party for some locals in town with the invitations reading, "You are invited to a Wedding...maybe even your own!"

VIGNETTES

SOME OTHER STORIES
IN A SERIES
OF ONE MILLION

Potty Prose

At one time we had two guitar players who strolled and played for the guests in the dining room. They always started in the middle of the evening because we only allowed them to play for the second seating, as we needed the tables turned over from the first seating.

When they first came in for the evening, the guitar players would go downstairs by the men's room and they would store their guitar cases in the wine room, which is right opposite the men's room, at the bottom of the steps. They would then stand right outside the men's room warming up on their instruments. One night as I was walking around at approximately 8:30 p.m., a couple was walking out of the front door. The woman looked down the steps, saw the guitar players rehearsing, and said to her male escort, "Boy, is this place fancy! They have two guitar players in the men's room!"

W e have this great, black piano player who alternates with a white piano player. We also have a black, men's room attendant who works in a tuxedo and carries two attache cases to and from work, which hold his precious toiletries and whatever other amenities he uses to service his customers.

There is a certain "Big Spender" from the East Coast who has a condominium in Palm Springs, and who frequents Melvyn's bar regularly. One evening about 11 p.m., the "Big Spender" pulls up in the driveway, and as he gets out of his car with his lady friend, the men's room attendant is leaving. The "Big Spender" assumes he is the piano player and asks him, "Where're you going?" The men's room attendant says "Home." The "Big Spender" goes into his pocket, pulls out a ONE HUNDRED DOLLAR BILL, and says, "Can you hang around another hour?" The bathroom attendant takes a look at the $100 bill and says "YES SIR!" and runs right back into the bathroom, opens his attache cases, and lays out his brushes and toiletries. Now the "Big Spender" sees the white piano player and starts to look around for the black piano player. He goes down to the bathroom, sees the black attendant in the bathroom and says, "What are you doing here?" The bathroom attendant replies, "Well, you asked me to hang around another hour." With that, of course, the guy realizes he had tipped the toilet room attendant by mistake, comes running up to me and says "You'll never believe what I just did—I tipped the men's room attendant $100..." and tells the story. Thinking it was the funniest thing that had happened in quite a while, I told the story throughout the restaurant immediately. The next day when I came to work, I had five waiters' applications on my desk for the job of men's room attendant!

Cameron Mitchell and Hope Holiday, the famous Hollywood actor and actress became friends of mine through the restaurant, as they were regular customers. One day as they were entertaining some people in Melvyn's, I went over to the table and started chatting. Cameron was ribbing me about all the press I was receiving in newspapers and magazines as well as appearing on several national TV shows. I commented that with all I had done I had never appeared in a movie. Cameron turned to me, and more to impress his guests than me, said, "You really want to be in a movie? I am filming one now and I've a perfect speaking part for you." I got all excited and said, "Absolutely, I would love to appear in it." He asked me if I had a three-piece white suit, a lot of gold chains, and would they be able to film the scene in a corner of the restaurant. The white suit was no problem; I had bought one my first year in Palm Springs and only worn it once. The gold chains were easy enough to come by from some of the waiters, and the corner of the restaurant as the setting was easy enough to furnish. Cameron told me he was in the middle of filming and producing a movie called "Kill Point" and that it was being shot in the desert, and also had my good friend, Marc Lawrence in it. He said he had a part for me as a South American gun dealer and in the particular scene I would be making a "gun buy." He said it was a speaking part with several lines. I really got excited and asked him when the filming would take place, and he replied in approximately three to four weeks, and he would call me beforehand to set it up.

Approximately three weeks passed when I got a call from someone who identified himself as Production Assistant for the movie, and that they had scheduled the filming for the following day at 4 o'clock at Melvyn's. The

Production Assistant said I should have my gold chains, my three-piece white suit and they would bring in the script AN HOUR EARLIER so I could study my lines. I cannot describe how excited I was.

The next day at approximately 3 p.m., forty people converged on Melvyn's Restaurant...production people, actors, actresses, extras, cameramen and on and on. This really was exciting. The head of production told me that Hope Holiday and Cameron Mitchell were just finishing a scene in Indio and would be along shortly. They gave me my script to study and I was certain I was on the way to stardom. An anxious hour and a half passed with no sign of Cameron or Hope. At approximately 5 p.m., the person in charge of production received a phone call from Cameron, that their car had broken down in Indio, and they would have to reschedule the shooting for a later date. I was informed they would call me 24 hours before the reshooting. Everybody packed up and left. Needless to say, I felt quite disappointed and frustrated.

That was approximately three years ago and I am still waiting for the call to schedule the shooting. (The movie "Kill Point" was released approximately 18 months ago!)